TRUE STORIES OF WELL-MEANING MISMATCHES

"Have I GOT A GUY for YOU"

what *really* happens
when Mom fixes you up

Edited by Alix Strauss

POLKA DOT
press ®

avon, massachusetts

Published by Polka Dot Press, an imprint of Adams Media, an F+W Publications Company 57 Littlefield Street, Avon, MA 02322 *www.adamsmedia.com*

The Polka Dot Press® name and logo design are registered trademarks of F+W Publications, Inc.

ISBN-13: 978-1-59869-433-8
ISBN-10: 1-59869-433-2

Printed in Canada.

J I H G F E D C B A

Library of Congress Cataloging-in-Publication Data is available from the publisher.

This publication is designed to provide accurate and authoritative information with regard to the subject matter covered. It is sold with the understanding that the publisher is not engaged in rendering legal, accounting, or other professional advice. If legal advice or other expert assistance is required, the services of a competent professional person should be sought.

    —From a *Declaration of Principles* jointly adopted by a Committee of the American Bar Association and a Committee of Publishers and Associations

Many of the designations used by manufacturers and sellers to distinguish their product are claimed as trademarks. Where those designations appear in this book and Adams Media was aware of a trademark claim, the designations have been printed with initial capital letters.

This book is available at quantity discounts for bulk purchases. For information, please call 1-800-289-0963.

To my mother,
who, thankfully, no longer sets me up

To all mothers
who continue to want the best for their daughters

To the wonderfully talented women
who contributed to this collection

And to single women everywhere,
we're all in this together

ACKNOWLEDGMENTS

To my agent Jennifer Unter who, though married to
a terrific guy, was still able to laugh and appreciate
these stories.

To our terrific editorial team, Jennifer Kushnier,
Andrea Norville, and Katrina Schroeder, your careful
eyes and sense of humor were greatly appreciated.

To the fine folks at Adams Media for publishing a
collection we girls could be proud of.

And to the women who gave of their time, their
talents, and their dating stories. Thank you all.

Contents

contents

contents

contents

⚏⚎

INTRODUCTION

Your Man Is Not My Man

Alix Strauss

A few years ago, my mother coerced me into joining a coed basket-ball team. Not for the important reasons one might think—sum-mer was readily approaching, enter the swimsuits and shorts; the joy of teamwork; de-stressing after a long day—but to meet guys. "It's *the* place," she insisted, as she handed me an article from the *Times* on hot spots for singles, which she had laminated.

Against my better judgment, I went, thinking if it didn't work out, I could use it as ammunition for the next time she wanted to commandeer my love life.

During the game, while I was on defense, one of my team-mates turned to me, and sensing that I looked a little lost and confused—basketball is not one of my stronger sports—reminded me I wasn't guarding my man.

"Where's your man?" he insisted, running past me, the sound of clomping feet echoing in my head. "You've got to find your man."

Out of breath, I stopped mid-court, dead in my tracks, too caught up in his statement to move. After all, this was the story of my life, or so my mother has been telling me.

Mothers by definition are a bizarre breed, a mixture of good intentions, well meaning, and optimistic naiveté. Put those qualities together and the end result is a black, mud-like concoction that oozes into your life and sticks to your clothing. It's this thick mass that clouds their judgment when they set up their children with prospective suitors.

Like many mothers, it seems mine is making a full-time job of trying to find me a husband. She'll pry into anyone's personal life—long-term friends and those she has known for only five minutes—in the hope of fixing me up with someone's son. She has arranged many blind dates, unable to understand my disappointment and frustration in her selection and criteria. I've been picked up late; asked to go dutch; lied to about someone's looks, their single status, their age, their occupation, and, perhaps most importantly, their personality (or lack thereof). After boring nights of conversation during which I've had to instigate every sentence, men have walked me home, slipped their tongue into my mouth, and copped a feel on the steps outside my apartment building only to receive praise and a thumbs-up from my doorman.

Last year my mother fixed me up with a friend's son's friend. She saw no picture, and knew no real information except that he was forty and worked. A member of the CSI Unit she isn't. She swore Roz had told her, "He's absolutely fabulous and wonderful, good looking, and very, very tall." Note to all: no one ever says, "Well, he's rather unattractive, just completed anger management classes, again, and he has a head wound that just won't seem to heal." That said, I was picked up by a 5'4" manchild who looked about twenty and wore a black eye patch—a temporary flaw, he assured me. He didn't make a reservation and had no idea where we should eat. I made several suggestions, none of which appealed to Ol' Blue Eye. An unhappy face was made when the bill came, and he sighed deeply as he shelled out two crisp twenties. After a long, boring evening filled with meaningless conversation, he escorted me home, where I was able to make a quick exit.

My mother, like many others, seems to be losing her conception of what a good man is, along with her hearing. I have told her countless times not to give my number out to random men, not to show my book jacket photo to someone's aunt, and to stop whipping out recently published articles for people on the bus to read. Though I think I have made myself more than clear, my requests ultimately get translated into "Sure, please feel free to give my number to anyone, anytime, anywhere." Though her intentions are good, she just isn't getting it. Then again, neither am I.

Her latest attempt was rather disastrous. Told he was bright, creative, and funny—a self-proclaimed comedian—I was stunned when I opened my door and found a guy, skyscraper tall, dressed in ripped jeans and sneakers, with bad Jewfro hair—as my tribe calls it. Suddenly I understood why men on Jdate and Match. com wear baseball hats in their pictures. When he smiled, which at least was more than I got from the date before him, his teeth were crooked, inverted, and yellow. I put on my best fake grin, extended my right hand, and was met by a clammy dead-fish grasp. Not one for solid food, he had a liquid meal of three Jack Daniels and soda. "Sometimes I get nervous before a set," he claimed. "Drinking calms me down." Did I mention he was performing the following evening? I had the Advil and was home within the hour. P.S., he didn't say one funny thing all night.

She pulled a similar stunt when I was bribed into meeting the son of a stranger she'd met while playing bridge at a friend's club. Again, I was promised the world. This time my date was bright, looked like he had stepped out of *GQ*, and had no trouble making small talk. But looks can be deceiving. He talked about himself while we waited to order, told me over appetizers about the incredible deals he was responsible for at work, and during our main course, informed me that his last girlfriend, a former Ford model, had begged him to marry her—but at the time, he just couldn't commit. Thanks to the mirror he positioned himself in front of, he was able to see both me and himself while we ate. During coffee, he picked his teeth with the edge of the Sweet'N Low packet. Not only have I sworn off blind dates, but I've also switched to using Equal.

Not all dates have been bad, however. Steve was cute, smart, and charming. He was well dressed, well educated, and, well, gay. I know this because after our dinner at a lovely, small-but-intimate restaurant in the Lower East Side, he asked if I wanted to go to a piano bar. "Tonight they're doing a Sondheim medley," he said riding up on his heels, a little too giddy. I'll admit, I was charmed, I'm a theater fan myself, and at home I considered if dating him would really be that bad. How important is sex anyway? Later that night, alone in my room, a date with my vibrator reminded me that yes, sex is important. The *Will & Grace* fantasy can only last so long.

The straw that broke my single back came when, on the last date my mother had coordinated, I found out during dinner that he was married.

"It's only been for six months," he said, "and it's not working out. I've asked for an annulment but she wants a divorce." He shrugged. "Whatever." Ah, not only was he good at commitment, but a wordsmith at that.

When I repeated this to my mother, asking her why she didn't know he had a significant other, she responded with "I didn't think to ask?"

And there's the rub.

For my mother, my quest for a man who's *dimensional* somehow has gotten confused with *demented*. Sophisticated shouldn't connote serious. And astute isn't equal to arrogant.

These days, my mom thinks anyone who graduated from college and doesn't have a coke habit is considered top-notch. She doesn't understand that those who appear normal are actually on a heavy mocktail of antidepressants, embrace odd mating habits, and collect weird items such as mini Snoopy figurines— true story. When these are considered to be the crop's best, it's almost impossible to imagine keeping a positive outlook while meeting prospective spouses.

My mother has long entered the stage where she'd love to hear two voices on my answering machine, receive birthday cards with two signatures, and see me become permanently joined at the hip. She pictures me and my man reading the *Times* in bed, brunching with other couples on Sundays, and becoming a Norman Rockwell painting. But this look into the future cannot happen unless I find Mr. Right on my own. Me, myself, and I—between the three of us, something should turn up.

When I finally found my man on the basketball court, he was sweaty and dribbling—from his chin. Not a pretty sight. I took a photo of him from my cell phone to show my mother. She thought he was cute and asked, "So, did you make a date?" I rest my case.

It's no secret that, as a culture, we've become dating obsessed. And blind dates, unfortunately, are a sorry part of it. There are no rule books to guide us through the dating drudgery. No list of helpful hints. No boy-scout preparation kits we can pack. On the whole, they're a level of hell Dante forgot to discuss in the *Inferno*. And that's where this book comes in. The 26 personal essays enclosed here are, unfortunately, all true. And since there are no twelve-step programs and no meetings for Victims of Bad Set-ups by Mothers for us to attend, this is our only way to vent and share our stories of misfortune. Humorous and heartfelt, we hope you'll feel part of a sisterhood of failed fix-ups, made worse by you-know-who. Like a support group to carry around in your Prada purse, these narratives let you in on the date while introducing you to each author's mother. They are funny, sad, and amusing stories, providing validating, tangible, and sympathetic proof that you are not alone—but rather in good company. And for you lucky few who have been spared the mother-induced fix-up, we hope you'll count your blessings while still enjoying the read.

A note to the Mothers of America, some words of caution: Please, please, please give your beloved daughters some time. Do not mistake our singleness for unhappiness, loneliness, or dysfunction. Don't tsk-tsk us or show pity. Don't delve into your Smythson black books or your blackberrys to find us a name of someone's friend whose son has a friend who still lives at home or with his fraternity brothers. Don't define our happiness by the person on our arm, or that our arm might be momentarily bare, like our ring finger. I swear, we are okay. Even happy. Our spouse will turn up. They do exist. We may not be sure where, but they're definitely out there. As history will prove in these essays, your Mr. Right is often our Mr. Wrong.

P.S., We still love you, we just need a little rest.

Letters to Gelman

Brenda Scott Royce

Dear Mr. Gelman,
It has come to my attention that you are single. As the producer of
a successful television show, you are just the type of man I'd like my
daughter to marry. She's a writer living in Los Angeles—smart, career-
minded, and attractive. I'm enclosing a photograph along with her
telephone number. Please call between the hours of 6 and 8 P.M.
—Phyllis in Florida

My mother is not crazy. I want to make that clear, right off the bat. I don't care what the clinical diagnosis is or whether her extreme matchmaking efforts would qualify her for "legal insanity" status in fourteen states. Given the right motivation, the most bizarre actions can be justified. Like her long-running attempts to fix me up with Michael Gelman, the then-single producer of the morning show *LIVE with Regis and Kathie Lee.* (This was long before Kelly Ripa came aboard as Regis's cohost and before Gelman married entertainment reporter Laurie Hibberd.)

Despite my insistence that I could manage my love life without her interference, and despite my far-out claim that few TV producers actually scrounge for romantic prospects in the viewer mailbag, my mother pressed on, prompted by Regis's on-air riffs about Gelman's single status, sending letter after letter to the morning show. While on the outside my mother's dogged persistence in trying to snag Gelman as a son-in-law might seem irrational—perhaps even borderline delusional—I like to believe it was just a case of maternal devotion gone awry.

I was working as an associate editor and taking night classes at a community college when my mother and I entered what I now refer to as our "Gelman Period." It began with a phone call one evening as I was studying for finals.

Upon hearing her voice, I said, "Hi Mom. What's his name?" This had become my standard greeting for my mother. She never failed to respond with a name, occupation, and personal stats ending with "and he's *single*."

"You think you know me so well," my mother said. "Did it ever occur to you that I might be calling to wish you well on your exam tomorrow?"

"Nope. What's his name?"

"It just so happens I love you and I want you to be happy."

"I know you do," I said. "What's his name?"

"Why are you so snippy?"

"I'm cramming," I said.

"Oh," she said, sounding relieved. "A little Midol should take care of that."

"*Cramming*, not cramping," I corrected. "Now what's his name?"

She exhaled dramatically. "Patrick. And hear me out this time. He's thirty-two and works as a mail carrier. Government benefits, you know. He's tall—"

"I don't want to be rude, Mom, but these fix-ups never work."

"That's because you're too picky. You want a man who's attractive, smart, has a good job, is nice to dogs, and has a super-hero cape in the closet."

"Don't exaggerate. I have my standards, that's all."

"Standards no mere mortal will ever meet." She sniffed. "Remember Craig? He was perfect."

Craig was a handyman my mother had met at Home Depot. Broad-shouldered with chiseled features, he was nice on the eyes, but we had nothing in common. I shuddered, remembering our tortured dinner conversation when we touched upon everything from classic cars to classical music and failed to find any common ground.

"He thought *Rigoletto* was a kind of pasta," I pointed out.

"Horrors," my mother mocked. "What about that philosophy student?"

"Jon? He spent our entire date trying to convince me I don't exist."

"Well, maybe you don't."

I sighed. "Give it up, Mom."

"I can't," she said. "I want you to be happy."

"I *am* happy. My career is taking off, I have great friends, I love living in L.A.—"

"But you're not *maaaarried*," she whined.

I found it ironic that my mother equated marriage with happiness, as she was the happiest person I knew and she'd been divorced since I was seven. A nurse by profession, she raised her four daughters to be independent and self-sufficient. Under her tutelage, my sisters and I each learned how to change a flat tire, build a bookcase, and balance a checkbook at an early age. She urged us to follow our dreams, see the world, and embark on exciting and challenging careers. But deep down, what she wanted most was for each of us to find a man, get married, and make babies.

When I was still single at thirty, she cranked up her matchmaking attempts. My sisters were married, so I was the sole target of her efforts. She'd chase men down in the pizza parlor or post office to pass out my number. I received many phone calls that began, "You don't know me, but I met your mother in Albertsons. . . ."

I usually declined these dates, but occasionally went along out of boredom, curiosity, or desperation. I agreed to meet one guy at a country western bar. I found him at a table right near the band. The music was deafening. On a break between songs he told me, "I picked this place so if you turned out to be a dog, at least I could listen to the music." He took a gulp of his beer and added, "but you're not a dog."

Gee, thanks.

I repeated this to my mother.

"Fine," she huffed. "Have it your way." Then, almost as an afterthought, she said, "But you should know, I sent your picture to Gelman. You know, from *Regis and Kathie Lee*."

I gasped. "I'm not doing one of those live makeovers, so you can just forget it."

"No, silly. He's single. And Regis thinks it's about time for him to settle down. So I sent him your picture." I felt a stabbing pain in my temple as she went on and on about how nice it would be to have a television producer in the family and wondered whether Regis and/or Kathie Lee would come to the wedding. "I told him to call after 6:00, so you'll be home from work," she concluded. "But before 8:00, because it's just not polite to call someone after 8:00 P.M."

I sighed. "He's not gonna call, Mom."

"Of course he will. I sent your picture. The one you had taken when you were trying to be an actress." The fact that the photo had failed to garner me any acting assignments didn't deter her from thinking it would land me a husband.

"But he lives in New York."

"So? He can afford to travel. And you live in L.A. He's probably there all the time on business. Oh my gosh—"

"What is it?"

From the level of alarm in her voice I thought the kitchen curtains must have caught on fire. But instead, she said, "I forgot to tell him about the time difference!"

I rolled my eyes. "He knows about the time difference, Mom."

"I have to go write a letter," she said before disconnecting.

Dear Mr. Gelman,

In my earlier letter (see photocopy, attached), I neglected to mention that the best time to call my daughter is between the hours of 6 and 8 P.M. Pacific Standard Time. That's a three-hour difference, as you're probably aware. I'm enclosing another photo of my daughter, as the black-and-white headshot I sent previously doesn't truly do her justice. This one was taken at the beach last summer.

—Phyllis in Florida

My mother would dutifully copy me on each letter she sent to Gelman, so that I would know what to say when he called. But months passed with no phone call.

"Just give it up, Mom," I said when the frequency of her letters verged on fanatical. "Save yourself the postage."

She huffed. "Why? Don't you think he's attractive? And intelligent?"

"I guess." I shrugged. "He doesn't say much on the show."

"Regis doesn't let him get a word in edgewise," she agreed. "Maybe I'll write to him about that."

I groaned in protest. "Listen, Mom, it doesn't matter what I think about him. He's not going to call me."

"Of course he will," she said. "Stop selling yourself short."

Our conversations during the Gelman Period followed a predictable pattern. I'd list reasons why I wasn't sitting by the phone waiting for him to call—reasons based on my having both feet firmly rooted in reality—and she'd counter with a pep talk geared toward convincing me I was good enough, smart enough, and pretty enough to date any TV producer I doggone pleased.

"That's not what I mean," I said. "There are tons of single women in New York. He's not going to date someone who lives in L.A."

Dear Gelman,

You have still not contacted my daughter, whose admirable qualities I have outlined in my previous letters (see photocopies, attached). Your reticence is understandable, as long-distance relationships can be difficult. I'm certain she would relocate in order to get to know a smart, successful, marriage-minded man like you. I am once again enclosing her phone numbers and another picture, in case you have misplaced my prior correspondence.

—Phyllis in Fla.

My nine-to-five job prevented me from watching *Regis* with any regularity, but after tuning in on a sick day I called my mother again. "Um, Mom? I saw Gelman on *Regis* today. I think he's Jewish."

"So? You're not anti-Semitic all of a sudden, are you?"

"Of course not. But he's looking for a nice *Jewish* girl—"

"That's it!" She hung up and fired off another missive, this one by e-mail, as she had recently purchased her first computer.

> *Gelman,*
> *She'll convert.*
> *—Phyl*

Her persistent, fervent belief that Gelman should—and would—call did not prevent my mother from pursuing other matrimonial prospects on my behalf. When I declined to go out with a patient's sister's former gym teacher, she muttered something about not putting all of one's eggs in one basket. If I shared my eggs with all the baskets she sent my way, I'd be busier than the Easter Bunny.

During a lull in the Gelman Period, I agreed to meet another of my mother's friend's neighbor's something-in-law, a massage therapist who had recently moved to L.A. My mother insisted it wasn't a fix-up, but a favor to someone who was new to town, and I reluctantly agreed.

We had been seated just a few minutes when a waiter arrived with two plates heaped with steaming food. I protested that he had the wrong table—we hadn't even placed an order yet—but my date informed me that he had taken the liberty of calling ahead so our food would be ready when we arrived.

"You ordered for me?" I asked, stunned. We'd never discussed our culinary likes or dislikes. How could he possibly know what I'd want to ingest at a restaurant I'd never been to? He smiled and explained that based upon our brief phone conversation, he'd intuited the perfect meal for my palate and temperament.

I stared at the plate in front of me, wondering what it was about my temperament that had suggested a slab of fish on wilted lettuce. "What is it?"

He smiled. "Scrod."

I wrinkled my nose. "I'm allergic to scrod."

He rolled his eyes and took a bite of his own entrée. "No one's allergic to scrod."

"I am," I said defiantly, pushing the plate aside. "I'm scrod intolerant." In truth, I have no food allergies, but I was standing on principle. There was no way was I getting scrod. I was prepared to live an entirely scrod-free existence rather than take a single bite.

Having to wait for another entrée to arrive while his got cold didn't dampen his enthusiasm for the date. As we ate, he boasted of psychic abilities, which he then tried to demonstrate without success, becoming increasingly frustrated as he incorrectly guessed both the number and suit I'd picked from a deck of cards. His claim that he could bend a spoon without touching it proved similarly unfounded.

Finally, he said he could cause any cloud in the sky to move using only the powers of his mind.

"But if you stare at any cloud long enough, eventually it will move," I pointed out as we walked to a nearby park and sat on a bench, looking up at the cloud-filled sky. The air was still, and after five minutes the cloud he'd pinpointed hadn't drifted even minutely.

I knew my mother would call that night—and I don't even claim to have psychic powers. And when she did the first thing she said was, "He told me you've got too much negative energy." She'd gotten her friend's report of the encounter. "It was blocking his abilities. Maybe that's why Gelman hasn't called yet. You're giving off negative vibes."

The Gelman Period officially came to a close when he announced his engagement to an entertainment reporter who, in my mom's estimation, must have had a more persuasive mother. Considering the amount of time she'd invested into cultivating him as a prospective son-in-law, I thought she took the news well.

Dear Mr. Gelman,

Congratulations on your recent engagement. While I have grave reservations that a union undertaken in haste—without due consideration of all options—will succeed, I nonetheless wish you well. Perhaps your new wife will help you develop the manners you currently lack, as evidenced by your inability to show my daughter the common courtesy of a phone call. I respectfully request that you disregard my previous correspondence (see photocopies, attached) and discard any photographs of her you may still have in your possession. Even if your current relationship does not work out, please refrain from contacting me or my daughter.

Sincerely,
Phyllis in Florida

P.S., I understand your fiancée intends to convert to Judaism before you marry. You may recall I suggested my daughter's willingness to do the same. Perhaps that's where you got the idea?

The same year—with no maternal intervention whatsoever—I met my husband. No cross-country relocation or religious conversions were required. In her unabashed affection for her son-in-law, my mother has conveniently forgotten her once-zealous attempts to marry me off to anyone else. But while she can dismiss the Cloud Mover and the You're-Not-a-Dog Dude as products of my overactive imagination, thanks to a bundle of photocopied letters gathering dust in my garage, we'll always have Gelman.

Vodka Honey, Straight Up

Leora Klein

Dan sounded great on paper: Upper East Side, Fieldston, Brown undergrad, NYU Law, formerly a corporate lawyer, currently CEO of a nonprofit that seeks to foster peace between Palestinian and Israeli children. . . . My mother met his mother at a charity dinner. Seated next to each other, nibbling on raisin nut rolls, patiently waiting for their salad plates to be whisked away, they noticed that neither woman ate the shaved fennel. By the time the blackened sea bass was served they were dear friends. She didn't wait for dessert to show my mother a photograph of her son, and my mother called me from the car on her way home to tell me the great news.

"She had a photograph of her son in her evening bag?"

"Actually, she had it on her cell phone, and he looked very handsome with a nice head of hair."

"Did you inquire about his height?" I am 5'9".

"I did and she said he was taller than her husband, and her husband was tall."

He sounded too perfect. My mother always taught me perfect doesn't exist.

"Did she mention his homosexual past?"

"Leora, don't be outrageous. He's not gay. I gave her your number. Please be open-minded when he calls."

I am open-minded. Past blind date suitors have been an eclectic mix of losers, Rhodes Scholars, closeted gays, dumb hotties, and very smart perverts. There was the guy who was small enough to fit in a teacup. He picked me up on his moped and my doorman couldn't stop laughing. One guy told me his SAT scores were no better than Forest Gump's. Another—with man boobs—referred to himself as a "poopy doctor" and told me, "if it's itchy with discharge, it's never good." Another wanted to watch the Paris Hilton video together and then make our own. The latest referred to Jessica Simpson's body in a text message.

When Dan phoned three days later, the conversation was breezy, and I liked his husky voice. His easy laugh. So I agreed to meet him the Wednesday night before Thanksgiving and picked a new martini bar around the corner from where I lived. Night set in very early by the end of November and our seven o'clock date felt much later.

As we met outside we did the awkward hello-kiss-hug-shake hands dance. He was over six feet tall with warm blue eyes and light brown hair. He wore a charcoal gray pea coat and broken-in tan cords. He was definitely hot, and I felt myself get good nervous.

As we browsed the cocktail menu, the waitress came over. Because it was the kick off to a holiday weekend, I ordered a fusion of citrus vodka, peach schnapps, and champagne. Dan looked up from the menu and said, "My throat has been bothering me all day. I think I'll just have a hot tea. And do you think I could trouble you for some honey?"

I instantly felt like a lush and debated changing my order to a coffee. But this was a date, and he was great looking, and it wasn't *my* throat that was hurting. The waitress said she doubted they had honey. "It's a bar, but I'll check."

I was annoyed with her for snapping at him and annoyed at him for ordering tea.

"I'm sorry that your throat hurts. A few of my students have had sore throats. I guess it's the start of the season."

"Where do you teach?" he asked.

"I teach eighth grade English at M.H.A." I replied.

"M.H.A.'s a good school. It's no Ramaz, but still a great school."

"Wait—did you go to Ramaz? I went to Ramaz," I said, slightly confused. I thought he was a Fieldston boy.

"No. But my ex-girlfriend did. So I know Ramaz."

Did I even want to go there? I didn't care for most of the people I went to high school with, and I didn't want the name of his ex-girlfriend to influence my opinion.

"You must know her," he continued. "Elyse Gross." He dropped her name like a stink bomb.

"She was a year ahead of me. Great girl. When did you date?"

The waitress dropped off our drinks. "No honey," she said and sauntered away.

"We dated for three years after college. I know she's married now and has a kid. I saw her in the park with this little blonde girl and it was really weird, for me. She was a huge force in my life. Had I been ready to get married, she would have married me. It would have been my kid."

"Where did you go to college?" I asked, trying to steer him in another direction.

"I was at Brown and she was at B.U. and we met at a party and we did the long distance thing for a semester but then we both graduated and moved to New York."

Dan was about to take his first sip of honeyless tea. But he put down the mug and blew into it. "It's very hot without the honey," he said. I nodded.

"I have a lot of friends that went to Brown. My roommate when I lived in L.A. was class of '98."

"You lived in L.A.? I probably don't know your friend. I'm class of '94. Anyway, we moved to New York and she got a place on the Upper West Side and so did I. I wanted to live together, but she wouldn't because her parents are Orthodox. Anyway, after three years, I wasn't ready to pop the question, so she ended it."

"Wow. That must have been tough. Do you still live on the Upper West Side?" I noticed my shoulders moving to The Killers's "Smile Like You Mean It." I stopped myself from singing.

"No, I moved to the West Village when I was in law school. I love it there, but I was living in my place with Megan, my most recent ex, so it still carries a lot of memories I'm trying to forget."

"Oh. I'm sorry to hear that." I took a quick sip of my drink. "Were you together long?"

"We were also together for three years and I wasn't ready to propose so we broke up. We had a very similar relationship to mine and Elyse's but it's still too fresh to discuss. I would prefer to use the Elyse relationship as the prototype."

Did he just use the word *prototype*? I took a larger sip of my beverage. "You know, I really don't—I think I'd rather hear about you. Tell me more about you. How did you decide to leave law?" I calibrated only three remaining mouthfuls of my cocktail. I'd need another round soon.

"Yeah, you're probably right. We aren't supposed to mention past relationships on a first date. I'll just say this: If you are looking to get married anytime soon, you got the wrong guy."

There's a place in a date when you just want it to end and you think that maybe draining the drink in your hand will be a visual clue that the night is over. I don't know if we had been there for more than thirty minutes, but I was done. Unfortunately, he wasn't. He waved the waitress over and asked for some more hot water. She looked at me and then at my empty glass. I wonder if she could see the desperation.

"I would like a vodka gimlet straight up, please. Belvedere." I announced.

"You got it," she said as she sashayed away.

I glanced at Dan, whose great looks had quickly deteriorated. His face had become creepy and mouthy. I didn't know what to say, but I knew I had to say something. I decided to unleash my own personal date poison.

"You know, Dan, marriage isn't in my immediate future. I was engaged once and I'm not running to the alter, either."

"You were engaged?" He put the mug down. "I guess that makes sense. You're a very attractive twenty-nine-year-old woman and by now someone must have tried to hold you down. I mean, something must be really wrong with you if no one had wanted to marry you by now."

If there was a compliment in there, I missed it.

"Not to say that something was wrong with either Elyse or Megan," he continued.

"You know, my throat really hurts. I hope you don't mind if I start transcribing my portion of the conversation."

Then he took out a small notebook from his coat pocket and clicked a pen with the name of his organization emblazoned in yellow and blue letters.

"Dan, why don't we call it a night if you aren't feeling well? I don't want to keep you out." But it was as if he didn't hear me.

Instead he wrote down, "No trouble. I really like talking to you and I'm a pretty quick writer."

The waitress brought our second round of drinks.

"So you want me to talk and you to write?"

He nodded.

"Really?"

He nodded emphatically.

"Okay. Well, nice pen!" I laughed. When he didn't, I wondered if I were being videotaped. "Tell me about the organization you started. It sounds wonderful, the little I know. My father is Israeli, and I remember when I was in high school my grandfather had a heart attack and his wonderful doctor was Arab and that positive experience has forever affected my perspective on the Arab/Israeli situation. I think if you make the political personal everything can change."

Dan looked at me for a long minute and then he shook his head.

After a detailed paragraph about his work, he flipped to a new page and wrote the following:

"Although I do think what I am doing is very important, it is difficult financially. When I look around at my friends who stayed in corporate law and IBanking—buying and selling their first and second apartments, flying to Aspen, dining at the finest restaurants—I question my timeline. Maybe I should have waited before I switched careers. I mean, I can't afford to send my kids to Fieldston or M.H.A. I feel very emasculated by my lack of finance. Part of me wonders if Megan knew—which is why she told me she didn't care about diamond engagement rings."

The good girl in me wanted to alleviate his worries and commend his choices. The sad girl in me wanted to run home, eat chocolate, call my mom, and cry. The bad girl in me wanted to pour honey in his pants and shout that no amount of money in the world would make his balls grow.

Instead, I took his pen and spoke briefly of my respect for his work, and then I excused myself. Once inside the safety of the bathroom stall, I realized I was good and drunk and still holding his pen. I had been expecting dinner and all I got was a belly full of vodka. I checked my face in the mirror. It was time to go. As I walked back to the table I discretely signaled to the waitress for the check. Dan must have had a little arsenal of ink in his jacket because he was writing, head down, over the paper, right hand moving swiftly across the page. For a brief moment I wondered if I was too sensitive or judgmental. He looked up and slipped the paper across the table to me. I couldn't bear to read it. I couldn't bear to see what his ink had spread.

"Dan, I have dinner reservations at nine, so I think we should head out."

He pointed to the note and the waitress dropped the check.

As I read a more developed take on finance and women and the culture of dating, I let him pay the bill. So what if all he had was tea? On the bottom of the page he had written two postscripts.

"P.S., thank you for respecting my choice.

"P.P.S., if I weren't feeling so ill, I would kiss you."

I looked up and half smiled. His cluelessness was breathtaking.

We headed outside into the cold crisp air (the kind that makes you think of stone fireplaces, cream cashmere sweaters, and good red wine). I told him I had to get a warmer coat before I headed to dinner. We walked in silence to my building and I thought about my parents. My mom married at twenty. She and my father have three kids, and they recently celebrated their thirty-fifth wedding anniversary. I am almost thirty (rhymes with dirty) and have been dating for over half my life. How, then, could I expect her to understand my twenty-first century love life? Why do I continually bring her into the folds of my heart? I seek her counsel and her confidence because she is wise and knowing. And isn't there something timeless about love?

Dan hugged me and I let him. I walked through my lobby, waved to my doorman, and slid straight into the elevator where I released my phone from my coat pocket. I wanted to wail against the unjust gods of romance and against the lame males who show up at my door and don't come close to the man I want and deserve. I wanted to wail at the wasted lifetime hours spent straightening my hair, putting on mascara, picking the right outfit, going to the dry cleaners, reading the business section, and getting so very hopeful and so deeply disappointed. I wanted to wail against the awfulness of it all and capture elusive understanding of how difficult this all had become. I exited the elevator, inserted the key in the lock, and hit send on my phone.

"Hi, Ma, it's me."

"How did it go?" The soft cadence of her Hungarian/Israeli accent made me smile. As I made myself some toast and apricot jam, I wondered what she could say that would make it okay.

"Oh you know," I offered, "only the worst date of my life."

"Really?" She sounded concerned.

As I made my way through the details of my night, we both just started to laugh.

"Let's just say, he isn't even perfect on paper," I told her.

The Monologist

Sara Barron

My mother is a fifty-nine-year old Midwestern Jew with a penchant for brightly colored socks, high-waisted jeans, and blazers from Talbots. Her taste in the men she thinks I should date mirrors closely her taste in fashion, which is to say, she's not discerning. Be it man or sock or sensible blazer, if it's there and available (because no one else would want it) *she's* interested.

On a cold Sunday a year ago, she called four times between seven and eight in the morning. On the fourth call I picked up the phone and she said, "You're never going to guess who I ran into last night at the movie theatre!"

"You're right," I told her, "I'm not."

"Between back-to-back showings of *War of the Worlds*, your father and I literally ran into Sharon Epstein! I'm reaching into my purse for my hand sanitizer, not watching where I'm going and suddenly: Boom! There I am! Face to face with her!"

Sharon was a friend from a water aerobics class my mother had taken. She and my mother got to talking and discovered they both had children living in New York.

"So I ask her 'What's new' and she says, '*My* son Aaron just moved to New York.' So I say '*My* daughter Sara lives in New

York.' *Then* it turns out you both live in Brooklyn! *Then* it turns out you're both *in the arts*"—"in the arts" is my mother's euphemism for "unemployed waiter with creative ambitions"—"*then* it turns out—guess what?!"

"Don't want to," I told her. "It's eight on a Sunday and I haven't had coffee."

She interrupted me by the time I hit the word "eight" shouting "You're both single!" She said this with the same kind of enthusiasm that most women reserve for a sentence like, "We're getting married!" or "His last name is Goldburg!"

"Anyway," she continued. "He's twenty-nine and a successful actor. A *musical theater* actor."

I knew that "successful actor," most likely meant "actor," and that "actor" most likely meant "waiter." And I wasn't thrilled with the "musical" part of things either. I knew it meant there'd be an eventual conversation about headshots, then another about jazz shoes, then another wherein he'd defend his heterosexuality to the extent that I'd have to question it. I vocalized these concerns to my mother who reminded me that I myself was a waiter—". . . a waiter," she was quick to point out "with an expensive college education paid for by your father and me which you seem incapable of using in the professional working world."

It was a fair point. And I would have told her so, had I been able to get a word in edgewise as she carried on for the better part of ten minutes, peppering her Aaron Epstein pitch with phrases like "fish in the sea," "beggars can't be choosers," and "not getting any younger."

Aaron called a week later and left a message that said: "Hi? Sara? This is Aaron? Aaron Epstein? Um, I'm Sharon's son and I guess our moms ran into each other? And my mom said I should call you? So I'm calling you?" Every sentence was a question spoken in a shrill falsetto.

I still returned the call because if I hadn't, he would've turned out to be *the one*; and because my mother would've harassed me about it for the better part of a year; *and* because I think it's unreasonable to judge people based on first-time voicemail messages—I know that when I, personally, leave a message for someone I'm anxious to call I sound like Ethel Merman high on an unreasonable amount of crack.

When we spoke in person, Aaron's voice had steadied—which was good—but he suggested we meet at Starbucks—which was not. He insisted on a dry locale because, as someone had failed to mention—my mom or Aaron's, I couldn't be sure—Aaron was, at age twenty-nine, a two-months-sober, recovering alcoholic. This fact alone didn't bode well. But, again: What boded worse was Starbucks. It's not at all that I require a four-star meal or a Tony address to get me enthused about a first date. On the contrary, I'm happy as a clam to grab a noncommittal, run-fast-if-you-have-to coffee or Earl Grey tea. But with hundreds of cozy, cute, and dimly lit coffee shops all over Manhattan, why we had to go to one with fluorescent lighting and a wide assortment of homeless people was beyond me.

We agreed to meet outside in front of the coffee house and to his credit he arrived early and first. Also to his credit he was—as my mother had promised—tall. That's how I'd known which one he was. What I hadn't prepared for was the head-to-toe leather ensemble: black leather pants, black leather jacket. It was as though having recently moved to New York, he told himself, "I hear that all the actors dress in black! That's what *I'll* do!" and then for whatever reason—either because he had the money or because he was retarded—he decided to do it in leather.

"Oh my gosh! Look at you! You own so much . . . leather!" I said, because it's the only thing that came to me.

His response, "Oh yeah. Totally," preceded an awkward five second silence which I broke with, "So, hi, by the way. I'm Sara."

"Oh yeah, totally," Aaron said again, extending his hand to shake, "I'm Aaron."

We went inside for tea (me) and mocha (him).

Things didn't go so smoothly with Aaron. He went before me in line, ordered his mocha, reached for his wallet, and realized he had a single dollar on him. "Oh shit," he said, "I've got, like, a buck, dude. Can you spot me?"

"Spot" may not have been the proper term: It suggested I'd get paid back. But it seemed too soon for a first fight, so I kept my mouth shut, laid down a ten, and walked tea-in- hand ahead of him toward the only open table, one adjacent to the public restroom. We sat there sipping our drinks and struggling through awkward silence between a group of skater teens—two with pierced cheeks and the third with a tattoo on his forehead that read, "What YOU lookin' at Willis?"—and on our other side, two hard-of-hearing elderly women discussing the workings of their gastrointestinal systems.

I'd been on blind dates before and learned from experience that the best way to get over the awkwardness that plagues the first twenty minutes is to ask a question about the other person's job.

"My mother tells me you're an actor?" I said.

Aaron nodded. "Yeah, totally. Acting's pretty much my life. I eat, sleep, and breathe theater, you know?"

I didn't know—I reserve that kind of passion for *Dancing with the Stars* or a good Reuben sandwich—but I nodded anyway. "And you work in musical theater, is that right?"

Again he responded, "Yeah, totally," and then took my question as an opportunity to deliver a diatribe on the history of his acting training and career. "It started in 1991," he began, "when I went to see a community theatre production of *Brigadoon*. I was thirteen years old and I sat in that theater watching all that music and passion and energy, and I was just like, 'Yes! Totally! I am *meant* for that!"

I learned quickly that "Successful Musical Theater Actor" meant "has performed in a summer stock production of *Pippin*," and "recovering alcoholic" meant "chews coffee stirrers maniacally in a way that leaves a constant stream of saliva connecting his lip to his chin." Aaron carried on about his "craft," his "passion" and, as predicted, a pair of jazz shoes he'd held on to from his first ever dance class, and his most recent headshots.

"In fact," he said, "I've got some copies in my dance bag and I'd really like your opinion on which ones you like best." He reached into a mahogany tote with the phrase *Gotta Dance* inscribed along the shoulder strap, and placed two glossy 8 × 10s on the table.

In the first, he leaned against a brick wall pouting his lips like he'd just said the word "poo." In the second, he stood against the same wall, this time smiling and clutching a fishing pole.

"Why the fishing pole?" I asked.

"Have you ever seen the movie *A River Runs Through It*?"

"Sure," I told him, "years ago."

"I was an extra in that movie and the acting experience had a real effect on me. Fly fishing's become a passion of mine and my acting coach suggested that holding the pole would be a great way of bringing even more of me and my personality to the shot."

I didn't know what to say besides, *You may or may not be a bonafide homosexual, but you sure as Sherlock are gay in the fifth grade sense.* And, as the saying goes, "If you can't say anything nice. . ." and so I didn't say anything at all.

"And in the second picture, the one where I'm looking really serious," he went on, "what I'm doing is this acting exercise called 'substitution.' It's where you remember a particular event in your life so you can recreate the emotion from the event in an acting scene. So for instance, in that shot, what I did was I brought myself back to this one day when I was on vacation in Aspen and I was just, like, standing on top of this mountain looking out at the world, you know? And being like, 'Wow. What's it all mean . . . what's it all for?"

I was asking myself the same question: What *is* it all for? Why do we agree to meet strangers at Starbucks? Why do we think: We *could* hit it off? Why does a straight man have jazz shoes? And a dance bag? And why am *I* not the one who vacations in Aspen?

"I do really want your opinion," Aaron said. "Do you like them? And *if* you like, which do you like *more*? And why?"

I believe in being honest. I believe in being honest when it's convenient for me to be so, in instances like this where my honesty could facilitate a much-needed end to a conversation on method acting. "To be honest, they're not my cup of tea. But what do I know? I take horrible pictures. The flash on the camera always makes me nervous and so then I start sweating and my make-up runs into my eyes."

I thought he'd reflect on my comment, bristle at my candor and the anecdote about the sweating, pack his dance bag, and go.

Instead it prompted him to prove himself. "Okay," he said, "then tell me what you think of *this*." The way he said it, with such pride and aggression, I swear I thought he was about to pull his pants down. Instead he pushed his chair back, stood up from the table, rolled his shoulders and neck around to loosen up his back and said, "This is a dramatic monologue I've been working on with my acting coach. She says it helps to showcase my masculine side to the casting directors."

Then he performed a monologue—an excerpt from *Brighton Beach Memoirs* that included lines like, "What the *hell* is going on here?" and *"Get out!* I said *get! out!"*—in the middle of Starbucks. He solicited a round of applause from the two old women sitting next to us. They seemed to enjoy Aaron's presentation; I on the other hand did not. I didn't enjoy the performance because as it happens, I'm severely allergic to unsolicited monologue performances in public. While they don't cause sneezing or hives, when exposed, I do experience extreme and immediate vaginal dryness.

It was five in the evening, but I told Aaron I had a really early morning at the office the next day.

"I thought you were a waiter," he said.

"Yes," I told him, and thought about it for a moment. "I am a waiter. I'm a waiter . . . in an office," and I ran out the front door.

I went home and watched *Must Love Dogs* and *Under the Tuscan Sun* back-to-back on TBS, comforted by the fact that someone as pretty as Diane Lane has dating problems too.

Then my mother called to see how things had gone.

"Not well," I told her on the phone. "He totes a dance bag and dresses all in leather."

"In a gay way?" she asked.

"Is there any other?" I responded. And with that, she admitted I was right, got off the phone and forwarded me an e-mail with a link to an article about the progress being made in the fields of artificial insemination.

Shaadi Abhi Naahi

Anita Kawatra

Ma ishwar ka roop hoti hai. The Hindi saying translated as "mothers are next to God," is roughly equivalent to the English "mother knows best." The latter statement is a given for the Indians, far too obvious even for a cliché.

My mother is 4'10" standing at her tallest, holds three master's degrees and a PhD, runs her own business, and fiercely defends the most important right of a woman—a man. An Indian girl is not complete without a husband. She scorns my comparatively carefree attitude of "when it happens, it happens"; no need to think about it much.

Three years ago, when I was in my early thirties, my mother took my love life into her own hands—hands she deemed far more capable than mine.

It all started when I was visiting my parents at the end of summer. My mother got a call from her best friend, who was so choked with excitement that all she could manage to shriek over the phone was "*Shaadi pukki! Shaadi pukki!*" Translated, that means "wedding all set! wedding all set!"—the sweetest phrase to an Indian mother—at least to one who's talking about her own child.

To my mother, it was pure poison. She hung up, her face fierce. She turned to me and said in a low, bitter voice, "Prisha Auntie's *younger* daughter is getting married. Now I have to give them a gift. When are we going to get all the gifts for your wedding?"

Prisha Auntie then called my mother daily with wedding updates, asking often, with perhaps a touch of Schadenfreude, Hindu-style, about me. I heard my mother sadly respond several times, "*Shaadi abhi naahi.*" No wedding yet.

My mother then hounded me by telephone for weeks on the topic, finally sending me a letter. "We are your parents. We want only the best for you. We are proud of you. Your biological clock is ticking. You are waiting for a Prince Charming. You must stop waiting for a Prince Charming. There is no Prince Charming."

Following this charming missive, my mother, irritated by my lack of immediate action to find a husband, took drastic measures. Though I'd been trying to get her to use e-mail for years, she suddenly decided to enter the twenty-first century through the lens of . . . online dating. On my behalf. Without telling me.

Dating is not even the correct word for the Indians. The name of the site says it all: *Hindumatrimonials.com*. Indians get right to the point. Nothing about matching or harmony or the right stuff. They go right to holy matrimony.

To round out the picture, the profile wizard allows you to choose from five different styles of vegetarianism and fifteen different kinds of Hinduism. I didn't even know there was more than one kind. Under complexion, there were three shades of "wheatish." Let's not even get into the sections on caste and family values.

Her list for my husband was simple. I found it taped to her desk.

- Tall (*For Indians, this means over 5'8"*)
- Handsome (*See tall*)
- Went to good school (= *some education in the United States*)
- From a good family (= *they're not in jail*)
- Able to support you (= *rich*)

Of course, my mother wrote my profile. She posted it right before Thanksgiving. But it wasn't quite time to tell me. Much later, when I read it, the main thing I noticed was that my complexion was *gora rung* (fair-to-wheatish) and I was 5'5" (I'm 5'3"). In the parallel universe of Indian matrimonials, it's perfectly normal for the "boy"—single Indian men, even if they're forty, are "boys"—to contact the girl's parents and exchange particulars.

My mother's profile was a hit: Sixty-three boys responded within the week. She culled the list to about a dozen, corresponding with them and sending photos. Suddenly, she was the e-mail queen.

She carefully printed and stapled profiles and photos, sorting them into piles of suitability. This was the point at which she, in her divine wisdom, chose to inform me. There was a lot of yelling, a few tears, and more comments about the biological clock. Yet somehow she shamelessly managed to guilt me into a date. I insisted on only one.

"No problem," my mother said brightly. She selected the top packet from the pile. "This is the best one. He is BBC journalist. Prestigious. Cambridge educated. British. Very handsome. No issues."

For Indians, "issues" means "children."

I thought, one date. It might stop the madness. And who knows, I might meet someone interesting.

His name was Sanjay, and he already had my cell number.

Upon my acquiescence, my mother phoned every few hours to see if he'd called. She told me that I was too busy at work, and that was why he hadn't called. She said I should call him, and she'd give me his number. She'd already spoken with him. "Very well-educated. British." When I demurred, she told me that Indian men don't like girls who play hard to get. "American girls like Indian boys. They chase after them. Indian boys are used to that now."

Sanjay called. He did indeed sound BBC. Polite. Sophisticated in that sort of world-weary patrician way. He asked me where I lived and suggested we meet at a place nearby.

We were supposed to go out on a Sunday night in January. I was on my way home from a ski day at Hunter, plagued by mad traffic. I called him to say I was running late. He said composedly, "Why don't we do it another time."

I had made the mistake of telling my mother we'd made the date, hoping to get her off my back. She called me at 6:59 the next morning to see how it went. When I told her we'd postponed, she immediately called the boy to get the story. Then she called back to yell at me for going skiing.

"Would you rather I sat at home that Sunday for the eight hours before the date?" I asked.

"Yes!"

On a Thursday evening in early February, the boy and I met at Opia, a dark midtown lounge-y sort of bar on the second floor of a hotel. I dressed up in a short yellow leather A-line skirt with a fitted black turtleneck. I even put on mascara, which for me meant it was a really big night out.

He was waiting for me outside the door to the lounge. He recognized me instantly (from a surreptitious photo by my mother).

He extended his hand—"Anita?" pronouncing my name with the sharp English "t." He wasn't bad looking, and was indeed tall, for an Indian. He had a thick shock of black hair, with only a faint hint of greasiness. He wore a black T-shirt and a sport coat, and spoke in that crisp British manner that seems to impress most Americans and, for that matter, most Indians. He opened the door and followed me through, giving his name to the hostess. She took us to a small table in the dimly lit room, away from the bar filled with beautiful-people types. He pulled out my chair.

I sank down on the low, uncomfortable furniture as Europeanish lounge music played just a tad too loud. Everyone looked intense. His seat seemed higher than mine.

I smiled and opened the menu.

He leaned forward, his arms crossed on the table. "So, what are you looking for in a husband?"

I looked up, startled. Huh? "Oh! Well, um, I think I would want someone intelligent, and kind, and passionate about—"

"What are your core beliefs?" he asked.

"I think that people should try to help others who—" *What kind of inane thing am I saying? Think of something better!*

"How do you describe yourself?"

"I think I'm, um—I mean I try to be a good person and I—" At that point, I would have described myself as startled. I realized I'd spent zero time thinking about what I wanted in someone and admired that he'd put some work into this. Maybe I'd been too blasé about dating.

He leaned forward even more. I almost thought he was going to take my hands.

"What are your views on relationships in general and marriage in particular?"

"I certainly think that relationships are a positive—" *Where is our waitress?! What do I think about relationships? I'd like to have one!*

"How many children do you want to have?"

"Oh, I'm open to—"

Once again, I realized that as annoying as Sanjay was, staring at me intensely, self-righteously, drinking in my words with just a faint look of distaste at my deer-in-the-headlights responses, I was slightly horrified with myself for not knowing anything about what I actually might want from a relationship.

"Where do you want to live?"

Yes! I knew this one!

"I like New York, but I've always wanted to live abroad, perhaps in London or Paris."

Although this was the truth, I thought, even at the time, that it sounded so 1950s sorority sister, the kind of girl Sylvia Plath would skewer.

Please, no more questions. I hadn't even gotten my drink!

"Have you ever been in love?"

Caught again. While the questions about marriage and children were just a tad overdone for the first ninety seconds of a date, they were actually fairly conventional. No single woman reaches her thirties without having reasonably polite answers ready for fellow guests at wedding receptions. But this was personal. I wasn't ready for it.

Our drinks finally came. Unfortunately, mine was only club soda, as I was on yet another of my healthy living kicks. What I needed was a martini. Shaken or stirred, I didn't give a damn.

Sanjay sipped his Scotch and soda and tilted back in his chair, lifting its front legs a few inches off the ground intermittently pressing the tips of his fingers together in a stylized pose he had obviously picked up from an old movie.

"As a professional journalist for the BBC, I am preternaturally observant. My powers of perception are far greater than those of the typical person."

Oh, really?

"For example, I can tell that you really want companionship, despite your apparent success in life. I know that you had your heart seriously broken because tears filled your eyes when I asked you if you had been in love."

Excuse me? (But what I was also thinking was, *Did tears really fill my eyes? Am I that transparent?* Maybe this guy is really good at analysis.)

Then he sat forward. Elbows on the table, he leaned in even closer than before and told me what he was looking for.

"I want a woman who's beautiful and very flexible. I travel a great deal, and I need someone who is willing to move around with me and support what I want."

Okay.

"I want to have three children, close together in age, as that's best for child development."

Seems reasonable.

"I want to spend time in Europe and the United States, with a base in New York or London."

Check.

"What's important to me is threefold. I want to live a life filled with new experiences and challenges. I want to be a prize-winning journalist. I want to have a family."

Got it. You have to admire someone who knows what he wants.

"As far as sexual matters, I like to be adventurous in sex. I like it rough. I need someone who's accommodating, who's open to anything. I don't want anyone prudish or repressed."

Whoa, Nelly. We're twenty minutes into our first date! Part of me wanted to toss my club soda in his face—really just for effect. I wasn't angry—in fact, his depth of organization mesmerized me.

". . . someone who's comfortable with my taking the lead. With anything, whether it's voyeurism or being tied up or . . ."

I was stunned into stillness. I sipped my drink, speechless. The waitress arrived. He resumed his clipped voice and said, "We'll order dinner. What would you like?" I started out with a polite, "Everything looks good—" Without waiting, he turned to the waitress and said, "We'll have the endive salad, the tuna tartare, the salmon, and the couscous."

Actually, those all sounded pretty good. Was that rude or polite? He displayed impeccable British manners, ate tines down, and didn't talk with his mouth full. Over the next forty-five minutes he completed the section on sexual preferences—quite specifically, including number of times per week (four—except on vacations, then six). Then he moved on to finances, and how he will control who does what with how much. He wasn't interested in anything I had to say, but I was oddly enthralled.

I was still trying to figure out if things really worked this way when the waitress placed a leather case with the bill by him. He took it, glanced at the bill, pulled out his wallet, extracted his black Amex, and slipped it in the case, not missing a beat of his commentary.

Five minutes later, very correctly and with a formal stiffness, Sanjay walked me out of the restaurant, down the flight of stairs to the street, and then to the corner of 57th and Lexington. In no way was there any indication that we'd just had a heart-baring conversation. I stuck out my hand to make it clear I was moving on.

"Thank y—" I started to say, but he took me by the shoulders with both hands and kissed me on both cheeks—passionlessly, without a hint of affection.

I went home wondering, "Could this have possibly happened to anyone else?"

I didn't quite tell my mother the whole story. She could not understand why I refused to go out with Sanjay again. "He is such a nice boy!" she wailed. "BBC!"

My mom, ever pushing forward, then convinced me to try "It's Just an Hour," an "American" dating service. She said, "If you won't do ours, then you can do yours. Your dad and I will pay." I completed the profile myself, with the correct height and real-life hobbies, thinking, "Maybe I should spend some time figuring out what I want."

The service called me on the phone. "Hi, it's Linda from IJH. We have your first date!" Maybe it would be nice to meet someone.

"You'll be meeting at the Beacon on 56th. He's very well educated. He's a professional with a master's degree. I think he'll be just right for you. We don't do last names," she continued. "But his first name is Sanjay."

I didn't go on the date.

My Date with Pathology

Lois Barth

"Hi, honey, it's Mom," my mother's voice reverberates through my apartment as I retrieve my messages—like she has to tell me—"I met a lovely boy. Very virile. Found him at a health food restaurant during my lunch with Martha. What a bore! Not the man. Martha! But the man—very virile, a real salt-of-the-earth type. So, I know you don't approve, but you *always* trust my judgment. So I gave Victor your number."

My mother has her own language. I call it Jewish Morse Code. In her hidden catch phrases, all is revealed. I have learned that, "virile" means upright and without catheter. "Salt of the earth" means he's homely with pimples. "Lovely" means he's a momma's boy. Victor falls into all three categories. I'm in trouble.

The phone rings. It's Victor the Virile.

"Hello, I would like to speak to Lois," a deep voice resonates over the phone line. Hmm, not the nasal, fingers-against-the-chalkboard voice I'd expect.

After the initial introduction, Victor launches into a list of all the great things that my mother said about me and how lucky I am to have such a wonderful loving mom. I start to feel badly about judging my mother's behavior so harshly. After all, she just wants her "independent daughter to not be so alone." Is that so terrible?

He turns out to be charming and engaging in addition to being a wordsmith of sorts. It's clear: He gives good phone. He explains that he usually waits a day or two before calling, but due to the glowing review he knew I wouldn't be "on the singles market" very long. (Usually such a quick callback is a red flag of desperation lurking under the surface, but given the fact that I just finished a fifteen-month relationship with the most noncommittal man in New York City, I welcome his proactive gesture.)

Both of us are in the health-care profession. Victor works in pharmaceuticals; I'm a massage therapist and health care lecturer. We launch right into a playful conversation, using our working knowledge of anatomical terms to spar a bit, delighted by our shared anatomy speak.

He asks me out for lunch, and requests we go to the same health food restaurant where he and my mother had met. After an exclusive tour of all the Chicken-n-Ribs places during my last relationship, healthy eating sounds like a nice change.

After I hang up I think, *Hmm, maybe I'm wrong about my mother's instincts* and quickly drift into the world of what I call "you never know." You never know, maybe we can work together, he brings the medical piece, and I bring the holistic. You never know, I have always wanted a partner in both love and work.

I arrive at the organic vegan restaurant. It has a monastic vibe, with a short list of seasonings, and a long line out the door.

Due to his "medium height, medium build, medium brown hair" description I opt to meet him at the entranceway. The thought of having to endure the embarrassment of quizzing the long line of male diners as to whether or not they are Victor, is more than I can bear. Thankfully, the sight of his black satchel tote with the name of his pharmaceutical company on it saves me, which is truly a blessing, since he is literally indistinguishable from the other granola guys who are waiting to get in.

"Hey, what's up?" Victor says, clad in a plaid flannel shirt, with beige, wrinkled khakis and black Birkenstocks with worn through white socks. My expectations quickly plummet. This is not the Victor I visualized during our phone conversation. Priding myself on not being "superficial" when it comes to instant chemistry, I scramble for my optimism.

"Hi, nice to meet you," I reply and extend my hand. He reciprocates with this limp dishrag handshake that unfortunately matches his pallor.

As soon as we sit down I discover why Victor picked this restaurant: He is allergic to *everything*.

"This is one of few restaurants I feel safe eating in. I know the chef. I've toured the kitchen on many occasions."

For someone who feels so "safe," it surprises me to hear his unending inquiry (down to the trace minerals) of every dish. When it comes to special needs cuisine, he is more like a surly senior than a swinging single.

"What's in the steamed greens?" he barks at the waitress as soon as she approaches the table. I am slack-jawed. What the hell does he think is in steamed greens? The rice and beans combo brings forth a flurry of questions as well. Are the adzuki beans fresh? Is the seaweed crisp or limp?

I flash an apologetic smile to the waitress while he orders in a painstaking and obnoxious way. She flashes one back, clearly feeling sorry for me.

Ok, I rationalize, so he's eccentric when it comes to his food. Maybe he has some health issues and needs to be careful. But as the conversation progresses, I soon find out that his complaining is not limited to food.

"Can't believe the high prices of organic vegetables, it's enough to kill you," he says, letting out this ridiculously loud snorting laugh.

He then goes on a tirade about the level of sodium in tamari and how it aggravated his gout. I'm dumbfounded. There seems to be absolutely no correlation between the person I spoke to over the phone and the one across the table.

I fantasize about tackling the waitress and canceling my order. No, I'll go to the ladies' room and call a friend and ask her to call me on my pager. Just as I make my plan, I eye the huge yellow "sorry, out of order," sign on the payphone. You're sorry. This was before cell phones, so in terms of an easy exit, there is none.

I start to strategize an alternative plan but the terminally nice part of me intervenes and urges me not to hurt his feelings. The despairing dater in me counters, crying out, *Forget feelings—run, don't walk!* Then of course my mother's voice pops up telling me what a "slap in the face" it would be if I left before the meal. As I try to sort it all out, the food arrives.

I had ordered the quickest dish on the menu for the fastest exit. He, unfortunately, did not. As he dug into his Steam Bowl Deluxe, a colossal bowl brimming over with rice, beans, seaweed, and greens, he mentioned that he chews each mouthful twenty-five to thirty times in order to level out the alkaline/acidic pH balance of his ornery digestive tract.

So, for the next forty minutes, I endure loud smacking sounds coupled with excessive napkin use.

"Makes one so much more conscious of what and how they are eating," he proudly reports.

"Uh-huh," I respond, not knowing how to answer. One hour, I'm out of here, I reassure myself. Just get through it. But even though I am in pain, I decide I don't have to be in misery. "Waitress, dessert menu please."

Victor furrows his unibrow.

"Excuse me," I jump in. "Is there a problem?"

"Well," Victor shakes his head in a disapproving manner. "It's a free country. But no matter how you slice it, sugar in any form, is still sugar."

I think about fighting him on it, but when I see the vast array of pale colored sawdust textured *goodies*, I realize it isn't worth my time or the calories.

"Good, now that the *hard* part is over, we can get to the fun part of the date, an opportunity to make a connection," he says reaching across the table and grabbing my hand with a clammy grip. "So, how fascinating, you are a massage therapist and a speaker? Do you work in private practice? What modalities are you trained in? How did you get started?"

"Well," I begin as I pull away, "I'm also an actress and a solo-performance artist."

"Oh how funny, I'm an artist of sorts too, I play a little bit of guitar in the coffee houses, but ever since that damn carpal tunnel kicked in, I'm out of commission. Perhaps if things work out I'll 'let you' work on me. Do you offer any 'starving artist' discounts?"

I make a painful attempt to smile and just continue. "So I've always been interested in how the human body works."

"Mine's certainly not working so good these days. I had this horrible anterior cruciate ligament surgery that really gets to me," he rolls up his cuff and flashes me his stitches. "Here, palpate it, I'd love your feedback."

It's bad enough when guys try to grope you within fifteen minutes, but being asked to a feel his scar tissue?

Victor senses my discomfort and shifts channels. "Timing is everything. Like how we met. I'm sort of fatalistic that way. For example, my appendicitis attack back in '85," he trails off ready to launch into yet another discourse on his various ailments.

I cringe with the thought of what form of exposure was next. I switch the topic immediately. Anything benign.

"Speaking of timing, isn't this a beautiful time of year, what with the leaves turning and everything?" proud of my save.

"Beautiful on an aesthetic level maybe, but a real bitch on the allergies." As if on cue, he blows his nose with a loud honk into a wrinkled handkerchief that he takes out of his shirt pocket.

At this point I give up all attempts to steer our exchange in any direction and let him captain the SS *Pathology Star* toward our doomful dating destiny.

"You don't buy a Steam Bowl Deluxe, you just rent it," he adds, his charming way of excusing himself to go to the bathroom.

On his way back from the bathroom he decides to show me the exercises the physical therapist gave him, bending his leg while doing dips, clutching the side of the table.

I look at my watch and realize I've clocked in a full hour from the first quasi-handshake. I am ready to dart but he beats me to it.

"Wow, I'm really sorry. I can't keep Annasuya—my acupuncturist—waiting. The clock starts ticking right at 3 P.M. Boy, did this fly," he glows, limply shaking my hand, while we are still seated at the table.

The bill is lying face down in front of us. After much muttering, he reaches for the check and bellows "What the hell! This one's on me." I'm horrified as he removes a wad of balled up mostly dollar bills and counts out loud, planting each one on the table.

"Your mom, Edie, is such a great lady. I overheard her talking about her gallbladder operation. Boy, did we split a gut over the post-operative diet and the drafty pajamas."

After he pays the bill, we walk out and he plants a creepy peck on my cheek followed by a feeble attempt at a hug.

"We must do this again," he says, and leaves.

Was mother's criteria for fixing me up with Victor their shared maladies? Whatever happened to her old criteria of "kind eyes and well heeled"?

Later that day, I recount the date complete with impersonations. As she laughs an apology ekes through.

"Boy, what an *Alta cocker*," (Yiddish for feeble old man) my mother says. "I thought he was virile and that you'd have a lot in common."

"We do. He's got a condition. I have a treatment plan."

My mother howls.

"Do me a favor Mom, next time you meet another 'virile' type, give him my rates instead of my number."

Going Postal

Tracey Toomey

The circumstances were dire. I had exactly $27 in my checking account and twenty-four hours to move out of my NYU-owned apartment building. With no money and no apartment, I was forced to do the unthinkable—move home.

My bedroom in my parent's house was bizarre time capsule—pictures from my prom, the American Girl doll collection on a shelf, and posters of the cast of *90210*—and my mother hadn't changed a thing since I moved out four years before. That night I slept fitfully in my tiny twin bed; it seemed unbearably small after a year of sprawling out on a roomy queen. In the morning, I went downstairs to find my mother making breakfast.

"Good morning," she said brightly as she spooned yogurt and fresh blueberries into the blender. "Do you have anything going on this weekend?"

"Nope," I said.

"No hot dates lined up?" she asked, only half-jokingly.

"Mom," I countered, already getting annoyed. "I *just* moved home. How could I have met someone already?"

Deciding to ignore my question, she pressed the on button, and the blender whirled to life.

"I was at Justin Peters on Thursday," she said, switching gears, "getting my hair frosted, and Stephanie was asking about you." Stephanie was her colorist. A couple of years before, my mom had started getting her hair "frosted" every six weeks and as a result, she and Stephanie had become pretty close in spite of their twenty-five-year age difference.

"And . . ." my mom continued, "she was saying she wants to set you up with her brother, Gary. Apparently, he's adorable."

"Isn't Stephanie's brother married?" I asked.

"Divorced," my mom quickly pointed out.

"And doesn't he have kids?"

My mother sighed as she poured her silky smoothie into a scrupulously scrubbed glass. "Do what you want. I just thought it might be fun." She took a delicate sip.

Maybe it was because I felt indebted to my parents for taking me back in after they paid for four years of college, or maybe it was because I hadn't had a date since fall semester when I broke up with Michael, my boyfriend of over two years, but suddenly, I heard myself say, "Fine. I'll go."

The look of pure elation on my mother's face made my rash decision worth it.

"But," I added before she could get too excited, "I'll only go if it's a double date. I'm not going alone. I've never even *seen* him."

My mom clapped her hands excitedly. "Stephanie just started dating someone. I'm sure they'd love to go with you!"

A half an hour before Gary was supposed to pick me up, I was in my robe blow-drying my hair when I noticed my mom hovering in the doorway of the bathroom.

"You look beautiful," she said, handing me a small plastic bag from CVS. "I bought you some mascara." Translation: "You're a pretty girl, but you'd look so much more attractive if you'd only put in a little effort."

When I walked into my bedroom, I discovered she'd actually laid out an outfit for me on my bed like she did when I was in kindergarten. My patience was wearing as thin as the gossamer pashmina she had chosen to complement the tasteful, yet sexy "little black dress," and I was about to call the whole thing off, when I heard the doorbell. He was nearly eighteen minutes early! Hurriedly, I threw on the dress my mom picked out—I had no time to search through my closet for something else to wear—quickly checked myself out in the mirror, and then proceeded downstairs.

My mom was in the foyer greeting Gary, but his back was to me and I couldn't get a good look at him. Slowly, he turned around . . . and I nearly died. Gary was what my friends on the block used to call the "Hot Mailman." He was literally our mailman—cute for a mailman, but still! Even though he was dressed in a button-down shirt and khakis, I couldn't help but picture him in that silly uniform of Bermuda shorts and knee socks. My mom caught the horrified expression on my face and shot me a stern look, indicating that I was past the proverbial point of no return. Gary and I awkwardly shook hands, before walking to the car where Stephanie and her date were waiting in the backseat.

"Have fun!" my mom called after us.

Gary opened the passenger door for me and I climbed in. The car smelled like week-old McDonald's French fries and I was immediately reminded of the fact that he had kids.

"Hey, Trace!" Stephanie shrieked. Every time I saw her she had a different hair color. That night it was red with chunky blonde highlights. She introduced me to Tom, her date, who I'd learned from my mother was a Harvard grad student spending the summer on Long Island doing an internship at Stony Brook Hospital. He was really cute with slightly disheveled brown hair and adorable dimples. I felt like asking Stephanie if we could switch dates, but then remembered that Gary is her brother.

Weeks prior, when I decided I needed to move home for the summer, I lined up a job waiting tables at Aqua Room, an upscale restaurant in my hometown. I suggested that the double date take place there so that I'd have home-court advantage.

"Why don't we get a drink at the bar first?" Tom suggested once we arrived. "Definitely!" I answered too eagerly. I ordered a Mount Gay and soda (my official summer cocktail) and as the rum settled warmly in my stomach, I gained fresh perspective. *Who cares if my date is the Hot Mailman?* I thought. *At least he's not the short, fat, balding UPS guy. I'm here and I might as well make the best of it.*

The hostess showed us to our table and Gary pulled out my chair for me. "How am I doing?" he asked sheepishly.

"What do you mean?" I replied.

"Well, it's my first date since the divorce, so I'm kind of out of practice." The sheer discomfort of our exchange made me squirm.

"You're doing fine," I stammered. A waitress who I'd met a couple of times at weekly staff meetings came over to drop off the menus and the wine list. I smiled at her lamely and seized the opportunity to order another cocktail.

"Was it hard getting Jackie to sleep tonight?" Stephanie asked Gary.

"Impossible," Gary answered, smiling and shaking his head. "When she found out the babysitter was coming, she lost it. She really hates when I go out."

I didn't say anything because I had nothing to add to this conversation. I didn't know the first thing about having kids. I was twenty-two and could barely take care of myself.

"Jackie is my four-year-old," Gary explained to me. "I also have a son, William, who's six. I can't wait for you to meet them." *Whoa! Who said anything about meeting the kids?* We hadn't even sampled our appetizers yet, and he was already making plans for me to join the family.

"Red or white?" Gary asked.

"Red," I answered, still reeling from the thought of me as a potential stepmom.

"Red for me too," Tom answered.

"I kind of feel like white," Stephanie said.

"Why don't we get a bottle of each?" Gary suggested.

"Perfect," I answered, thinking just keep the booze coming. *Why on earth would my mother think it was a good idea to set her twenty-two-year old up with a* father? I thought irritably.

The waitress came back to deliver the wine, and to take our order. I took a sip of the velvety Pinot Noir, which tasted like chocolate-covered cherries, and forced myself to relax.

"So," Gary said, "Stephanie tells me that you just graduated college. Congratulations."

"Thanks." I forced a smile.

"What was your major?"

"Drama," I answered.

"So you want to be an actress?"

I hated this question, because it implied that I wasn't already an actress. That I was just a waitress who lived at home with her parents. "Yes," I said.

"That's great," he responded. "I always wanted to go to college, but I never got around to it."

"So, what do you do?" I asked Gary, even though I already knew the answer. I just couldn't think of anything else to say.

"I'm a postal worker," he replied. "You're house is on my route."

"You're kidding!" I exclaimed, hoping my BFA in acting was serving me well.

"Tracey," Stephanie interrupted abruptly. "Come to the bathroom with me."

"I think it's just a single," I responded.

"So?"

An awkward pause followed. "Okay," I said finally, somewhat relieved to leave the table. Stephanie and I walked through the restaurant, past the kitchen where garlic and olive oil fumes escaped every time a waiter burst through the swinging double doors. She opened the bathroom door and walked inside, gesturing for me to follow.

I went in, figuring she probably just wanted to grill me about whether or not I liked her brother. But as soon as we were inside, she locked the door and pulled a tiny bag of cocaine out of her purse. She deposited a pea-sized amount on the webbing between her thumb and forefinger and inhaled. Then she deposited another dollop on her hand and held it out toward me.

"No thanks." My friends back in college used to call me the Virgin Mary because I never did drugs or smoked. I never even had a drink until the end of my freshman year. I wasn't about to start snorting some white powder with my mom's hairdresser in the bathroom of the restaurant where I worked.

"Why not?" she fired back.

"I just don't want to," I said, feeling like the heroine in a low-budget after-school special.

"What's your problem?" she demanded, belligerently.

Then, out of nowhere, she grabbed the back of my head and started kissing me—with tongue! I pulled away in shock, knocking the bag of coke all over her, and rushed out of the bathroom and into the kitchen where two bus boys were filling ramekins with butter. I stood there to catch my breath, before grudgingly returning to the table where everyone was eating their dinner. Stephanie barely looked up when I sat down. Moments later the waitress, God bless her, came over and dropped our check. Not even waiting to finish my tuna tartar, I reached for my wallet, but Gary insisted on paying for me.

"Why don't we go across the street to Napper Tandy's for another drink?" Tom suggested.

"No!" I blurted out, then recovered, "I, um, have to wake up really early tomorrow and don't want to be out too late. Sorry."

Gary patted my leg under the table and then rested his hand on my knee. My entire body stiffened. Then, just when I thought things couldn't get any weirder, Stephanie started stroking my *other* leg. I was getting fondled by both siblings at the same time! I looked over to Tom who was completely oblivious to the drama unfolding underneath the table. Just my luck that the only person who wasn't touching me was the one I actually found attractive.

After the credit card slips were signed, we were walking back toward the car when Stephanie said, "Tom, why don't you ride in front? Tracey can ride in back with me."

The idea of being squished next to Stephanie in the backseat of Gary's tiny 1986 Toyota Camry was enough to make me want to throw up my dinner. Gary helped me crawl into the miniscule backseat. As I settled in, I felt Stephanie's hand stroking my leg. I inched away from her grasp as Gary, who was driving, reached from his seat and squeezed my other leg. The eleven-minute ride home felt not unlike Dante's description of his voyage through the nine circles of hell.

As soon as the car pulled into my driveway, I tried to bolt, but being that it was a two-door car, I had to wait for Gary to get out before I could emancipate myself. "Goodnight," I called, starting to flee up the driveway.

"Wait a minute," Gary said, clutching my hand. "Let me walk you to the door."

"Okay," I said, inwardly cringing.

At my stoop, he leaned in and kissed me. Almost as soon as our lips met, I pulled away. Awkwardness hung in the air like a thick fog.

"Thanks for dinner," I stammered. "Bye!" I turned quickly and disappeared into my house as I came to the appalling realization that I'd kissed both siblings within an hour.

A couple of weeks later, I was waiting tables at Aqua Room when Tom came in for lunch and sat in my section.

"Hey," I said, placing a menu in front of him. "How are you?"

"Great," he said. "You?"

"I'm good."

"I haven't seen you since our double date," he said, smiling.

"Yeah. That was kind of a nightmare for me," I divulged. "Are you still dating Stephanie?"

"No," he said. "She was, uh . . . a little bit crazy."

"Yeah," I agreed, relieved. "Can I get you something to drink?"

"Actually, I was wondering what time you get off. I have tickets for the Yankees game tonight, and if you're interested. . . ."

"I'm a *huge* Yankees fan," I said excitedly. "I get out today at four. . . ."

Tom and I ended up dating for the rest of the summer. My mom took full credit for our relationship, telling everyone who would listen that she set me up with a handsome Harvard grad student. After all, she explained, I never would have met him if it weren't for her! Of course she left out the part about poor Gary. To this day, when I go home to visit my parents, if I see a mail truck, I hide!

Always a Bridesmaid

Leanne Shear

Many women I know started fantasizing about their weddings when they were little girls. Not me.

While my eight-year-old peers employed their Barbies for the Voodoo-ish ritual of "wedding day," I regularly gathered the same dolls and gleefully chopped off their flaxen locks, execution-style. Fast forward to when, at twenty-eight, I began my stint as permanent bridesmaid, filling the role ten times over the course of just one year. How could I help but be preoccupied—albeit for the first time in my life—with weddings? I'd been dating a guy named Matt for two years, but realized he wasn't husband material, so while I was witness to every exchange of vows this side of the Atlantic, I found myself untethered. My mom was incredibly supportive when we broke up.

After all, the mantra she instilled in me during my formative years included, "make a life for *yourself*," "don't count entirely on a man to make you happy," and "you have all the time in the world to get married—if you even ever want to at all—so don't rush!" Based on all that childhood indoctrination, I concluded she would be the perfect wedding date—good companionship, free hotel rooms (admittedly), and, most importantly, no pressure on me about being single.

During wedding number four, I found myself with Mom, sitting primly at the singles table—something with which by now I was more than comfortable—about to embark on the usual seven-course gourmet dinner. Just as I took an enormous bite of a buttered roll, she struck up a conversation with the guy on the other side of her. "So what do you do?" I overheard her ask, as I turned to the two guys on my right and struck up a conversation. As they told me how they knew the bride, I kept one curious ear trained to my mom, catching snippets of her conversation, which from the guy's end included "Harvard Business School," "private equity," and "bought an apartment." After having a boyfriend who was a professional bartender, living not even paycheck to paycheck but night to night, I couldn't help it when my ears perked up.

As if on cue, my mother turned to me and said, "This is my daughter Leanne. Leanne, this is Michael."

Perhaps a little overly exuberant about the trappings of private equity, I draped myself halfway across her to offer him my hand and get a good look, and right away I noticed his big, warm smile. He certainly wasn't the strapping, hot, athletic type, or alternately, the sexy, tortured poet type I usually favored, but overall, not too bad. "Nice to meet you," I said, flashing my most gleaming bridesmaid smile. His (small) hand, which came too far out of the sleeve of his slightly ill-fitting, yet expensive-looking, black suit, grasped mine. "Whoa! That's *quite* the handshake!" he exclaimed. I smiled, even though the shock of the just-caught-fishiness of his hand probably made it look more like a grimace.

"So," he began, turning his seat more toward me. "Your mom tells me you're a writer. . . ."

"Well, you two have fun," she interrupted, pushing her chair back gracefully. "I'm going to dance!"

"Your mom's great," Michael commented with another big grin, moving into her seat and leaning in even closer to me, adding, "She'd make the perfect mother-in-law."

I was distracted from the weirdness of his comment because at that second, I'd caught a whiff of his breath, which smelled like he'd ingested an entire package of mothballs. I pulled back as far as courtesy would allow and breathed out of my mouth for the next five minutes.

"Yeah, she really is," I responded sincerely, as the cadre of servers started methodically placing the requisite salad at the places of every guest—regardless of whether or not they were actually there. I picked up my fork and took a small bite. Meanwhile, Michael continued smiling and staring. "Yum, this is delicious!" I exclaimed, hoping it would spur him to pick up his fork, which he finally did. I thought about forcing myself to make conversation, even conjuring up something witty to say, then decided against it, taking another bite of salad.

I glanced around the bustling room—the huge crystal chandeliers seemed to reflect the excitement concentrated ten feet away on the dance floor: By now, most of the guests were ripping it up (Mom, of course, was in the middle of a group of my friends, bopping happily to the Motown band), and trapped at the table with Michael, I suddenly felt very alone. I prayed for her to return and save me. As if reading my mind, Mom suddenly breezed back to the table.

"So do you two have a date all set up?" she asked gaily, picking up her fork and dipping daintily into the chicken marsala that had just been set in front of us immediately after the salads were whisked away with military precision. Not exactly the kind of rescue I'd had in mind.

Michael laughed, absently rolling his diamond-encrusted gold watch around and around his wrist, and said, "We haven't gotten that far yet." As she walked back to the dance floor, he turned to me. "I was telling your mom that you're very beautiful, and she and I agreed you and I would really hit it off. Since we both live in New York, you'll go out with me, right," he stated. I was ready to kill my mom.

"Um. Okay, sure,"

"What about Monday?"

The sooner I got the date over with, the sooner I could commence not returning his calls, so. . . . "Sure," I said grimly.

"Great!" he crowed. "Now let's dance!" and with that, he grabbed my hand, practically yanking me out of my seat and onto the dance floor, where I spent the next hour casting dirty looks in Mom's direction over his shoulder.

At around eleven o'clock—about four hours before my usual time of wedding retirement, I faked a huge yawn, and uttered the transparent, "Gee! It's late and I'm beat."

"No!" Michael practically wailed.

I continued rapidly, "Yeah, sorry, I just have to call it a night. It's tiring being a bridesmaid!"

"Really?" he asked, looking at me meaningfully. "I was hoping we could have a nightcap."

"Mom," I hissed accusingly a few minutes later as we were leaving the ballroom together. "You can't do that to me!"

"Did you have fun with Michael?" she asked brightly.

"No!" I pouted.

"Leanne, why can't you let something *develop* into a relationship? Let it grow from just okay to fantastic!"

"But I'm not in the slightest bit attracted to him," I protested. Ugh, that breath. It wasn't like I wanted to be single forever, especially when all my friends were getting married. I just was never one to *settle*.

"I just think it's nice to find someone to go through life with. A partner makes it so much easier."

I couldn't believe how drastically she'd changed her tune from all those years growing up. "What? But you always said we never even had to get married if we didn't want to!"

"All I'm suggesting," she continued, "is that you give it a chance. Michael told me his father was the president of an oil company and he's very successful in his own right and, to top it off, is clearly crazy about you. Why not just have a drink with him?"

I sighed. My dating/relationship M.O. had historically been an all-or-nothing approach: If I wasn't madly in love with a guy from the first millisecond of our interaction, I wouldn't even consider going out with, kissing, or dating him. *But maybe that's the reason I'm always the bridesmaid*, I told myself. Plus, it certainly wouldn't hurt to get taken care of a little bit. . . .

When Michael called (for the fifth time) the day after the wedding to tell me he'd gotten reservations for the following night at the impossibly exclusive Waverly Inn, a cozy hot spot in my West Village neighborhood, I decided I was going to give the date a real shot. I crossed the threshold of Scoop—where I never shop, due to the astronomical prices and waify, coiffed patrons—and picked up a sparkly gold top and matching belt to go with my favorite jeans, spending the gross domestic product of a small country in about five minutes.

He was waiting at the bar when I walked in, wearing the finance guy uniform of a tailored button-down shirt, soft yellow cashmere sweater, pressed dress pants and shiny shoes, his long black cashmere coat (I couldn't help catching a peek at the label—Versace!) draped casually over his stubby arm. He came up to kiss me hello and even though his lips landed too close to mine, I refused to cringe. I'd also somehow forgotten that he was a good two inches shorter than me, and unfortunately, with me in my typical three-inch heels, we looked like Tom Cruise and Katie Holmes, in more ways than one.

We were immediately escorted to a table near the fireplace and Michael sat down next to me, taking my hand and edging closer still. I watched, feeling oddly violated, as his sausage-like fingers clutched mine, stroking each one individually.

"You look so pretty," he breathed, which was a mistake, because there was most definitely not any improvement in that department. Just like at the wedding, my resolve to give him a shot died in its tracks and all I felt was disgust. "I've been looking forward to our date from the moment we met."

Which was only two days ago, I wanted to say, but instead I murmured a noncommittal "mmmm" and looked out the window longingly at three girls laughing on the sidewalk, wishing I was anywhere but there. *How on earth did so many people end up marrying someone they weren't at all attracted to?* I wondered.

"What would you like to drink?" he asked, glancing at the menu.

"Wine!" I practically shouted. "Pinot Noir. How about a bottle?"

I used the opportunity to pull my hand out of his grasp and thumb through the menu. The waiter meandered over and Michael said pleasantly, "We'd like a bottle of Pinot Noir. Do you have any suggestions?"

"Of course, sir," the waiter responded, leaning over Michael's menu and pointing out a couple of options.

"No," Michael declared. "Those are all too expensive. Don't you have anything cheaper?" I felt the heat and color rise steadily up my neck, through my face and settle in my forehead. This guy basically told my mom that he *comes* from tons of money and *makes* a ton of money and he was haggling with the waiter over the price of a bottle of wine?

"Um, well, we don't have a cheaper Pinot, but there's a nice Syrah," the waiter replied haltingly, and then looked at me with what can only be described as sympathy.

"That'll be fine," Michael said, snapping the menu shut and turning to me adoringly. "Are you hungry, sweetie?"

"Actually, yes," I replied. I wondered why on God's earth he was talking to me like we'd been dating for years. "I can't wait to order!"

"You know, I was thinking," he began. "Why don't we just split a couple of appetizers instead of ordering entrées? The food is ridiculously overpriced here."

I looked at him incredulously, and then just nodded my head. Matt, my ex, might have been broke, but at least he was the most generous person I'd ever met—he spent every last dime he had on having a good time with me and his friends and family.

"I'll have the Tuna Nicoise salad," Michael told the waiter when he returned.

"And for your entrée?" the waiter prompted.

"That *is* my entrée. And she"—he said, gesturing in my direction—"will have the same."

"Um," I said feebly, feeling the urgent need to protest (punch him in the face?) but wanting the "dinner" to be over even more. "Yes."

"How was work today?" he asked solicitously, as another waiter came over to pour our wine. I quickly reached for the glass.

"Good." It was fast becoming evident that nothing was going to be more painful for me than making conversation with him: It was like his toxic breath and actions were poisoning the air around me.

"So, what do you want to do this weekend?" he asked, again reaching for my hand, even though I'd made every effort to hide them in my lap. "I was thinking we could. . . ."

I was saved from entertaining the notion of spending more time with him by the waiter's delivery of our "entrées." I sloshed some more wine into my glass and took a huge gulp, then plunged my fork into a piece of tuna, eating my paltry dinner as fast as humanly possible, no longer caring about propriety.

Michael took a bite of his salad too, chewing it loudly and grotesquely, his mouth open, and when his lips were done smacking, he put down his fork, leaned back in his chair, weaving his fingers together behind his head, and sighed happily. Then he turned to me.

"Hey! What do you think about getting a house in the Hamptons next summer?"

"Um, what do I think?" I asked, stalling. "What do you mean?" Was he asking me to get a house . . . with him?

"I mean, we should get a group of our friends together and get a great house! You mentioned you like Amagansett, and I'd be willing to branch out beyond Southampton if it makes you happy. . . ."

I almost laughed out loud. If I could help it, I was planning on never seeing him again, and he was thinking about getting a house with me months from now. I couldn't decide if he was appallingly presumptuous or comically clueless. For the sake of being a nice person, I settled on the latter. Right then, he put his arm around me and kissed my cheek, and I changed my mind. Fuck being nice.

Finally, *finally*, it was over, expedited by the fact that Michael refused all offers of dessert, coffee, or more wine. We gathered our coats and left the restaurant, and I fought the urge to sprint in the direction of my apartment. Instead, I said with all the grace I could procure, "Thanks so much, Michael. I had a really great time—"

"I did too," he said huskily, cutting me off. "I really feel like we have a connection, Leanne." Then he stood on his tip-toes, grabbed my face, and pulled it down to kiss me, essentially making my worst nightmare come true.

I was too shocked for a second to move, but when he softly moaned in my mouth with pleasure while kissing me, I snapped out of it and pulled away.

"You're right," he says. "Not here." He took my hand and started walking purposefully in the direction of my street. I silently dragged along behind him, not making eye contact with anyone, *He can't possibly expect to come up to my apartment, can he?*

Indeed he did. As I pulled out my keys and attempted to thank him again, he started to follow me into my building. I'd finally had enough, and wheeled around. "Stop," I commanded.

"What do you mean?" he asked, puzzled.

"Michael, thank you for dinner, you're great, but you're not coming up," I explained firmly, adding, "I'm just really busy with work and school these days and . . . I really think we're better off friends."

He backpedaled, his eyes sparking with shock. "I can't believe it," he said gloomily after a painful minute of just staring at me. The last words I ever heard from Michael were muffled by the heavy entrance door to my building: "But your mom liked me so much!"

I realized a couple of things that night as I gratefully entered my tiny studio and flopped down onto my couch. It's okay at times—even wonderful—to be alone; I don't need to force a relationship with a guy just because all my friends are getting married; and mothers may know "best," but instincts know better.

Monkey See, Monkey Suit

Katherine Wessling

My mother always made it clear I should get married, that I should have kids, and that places like church would be the likely petri dishes for these blessed events.

When I was in sixth grade, she started a hope chest for me—a special shelf in a cupboard in my bedroom where I could keep things I'd one day use to start my own home—useful things like linen hand towels from Ireland and embroidered cocktail napkins. Years before she had any grandchildren, my mother had an entire closet full of toys and clothes and books awaiting their arrival. But despite all that, there's only one time that she set me or either of my two sisters up on blind dates.

My mother is not a setter-upper. She comes from solid Midwestern stock—from a world where you met your husband at church or college, not at a bar or online. It was something that just happened—it wasn't proper to force it.

Like most mothers, she knew what was best for me. She wanted me to play tennis, because it was a "social sport," where I'd meet people and, later, suitable men. But I preferred riding my horse alone through the hills overlooking the Pacific, and in the Montana mountains that we'd visit some summers.

She ached for me to be a debutante, but that seemed girly and stuffy. She wanted me to go to the private all-girls school that my sisters attended, but I felt my life in West Los Angeles was rarified enough without spending my days surrounded by other privileged girls on the grounds of a former country club.

There were certain things I wasn't given a choice about: I did attend cotillion where Commander Unander and his wife, Mrs. Unander, taught me all about manners ("age before beauty") and the box step. But what I most remember is towering over boys whose sweaty hands left my white gloves soaked and overdoing it on the 7-Up and sherbet punch.

I learned early on that my mother's idea of what was best for me didn't necessarily coincide with my own. I often made decisions she disagreed with. Instead of attending the small, ivy-covered liberal arts college where my parents had met, I went to a large public university. Instead of wearing brightly colored coordinates, I often wore only black. "Who do you think you are, some kind of Bohemian?" my mother would ask.

However, when I was twenty-seven years old, I had cause to wonder, once again, if perhaps she did know best. I was living in New York, where I'd moved to be with Ian, the "love of my life," an architect who talked about light and form and wrote poetry. I was besotted. But he went off to work in Spain one summer and dumped me for a Spanish virgin. I was devastated. I'd cry in the shower late at night so my roommate couldn't hear, and cross the street without looking—not wanting to die, exactly, but not caring if I lived.

My mother, across the country, was so worried that she decided something must be done.

I was sitting in my dark cubicle in the aubergine and grey offices of the magazine where I checked facts, when she called to tell me that her brow stylist, Kiki, had a "great guy" for me to meet. She said they'd grown up together on Long Island; that he worked as a banker. "Come on, Katherine," my mother urged, "It couldn't hurt."

I hadn't had much luck with either blind dates or men in suits. I'd dated a series of them—bankers, lawyers, businessmen. Guys who talked about little but money—their media centers; their cars; their homes; their suits.

But my mother was trying to help, so I said yes.

Later that day, the phone rang.

"Uh, yeah—uh, hi. Dis is Sal. Kiki said I should call."

I'd only been in New York for a little over a year and I had some trouble deciphering his accent.

"So, a Cali girl," he stated.

"Cali?" I thought. "That's right," I said.

"Never been there. Been to Vegas. I love dat place!"

This wasn't starting well. If there was one place on earth I couldn't bear, it was "Vegas."

"Kiki says I gotta meet you," he went on. "When you wanna meet?" I wasn't sure about this, but I wanted it to work—I wanted my mother to be right. I said I was free on Thursday.

"Dat's great!" he said, "Where you wanna meet?"

I did a quick mental sweep of my neighborhood and settled on a low-key bar/restaurant near my apartment.

"I'm about 5'9", have dark hair, and I'll be wearin' a monkey suit."

I asked him to repeat himself. He did.

When we hung up I turned to my fellow fact-checker Rachel and asked, "What's a monkey suit?" which made her laugh.

"Where are you from? It's just a regular suit, you know, jacket and tie."

I showed up at the appointed time, 6:30 P.M., and found Sal standing outside in his monkey suit. He was around my height and had big brown eyes. I was thankful he looked nothing like tall, surfer-blond Ian.

"You Katherine?" he asked, chomping on a wad of gum.

I nodded.

"Oh, dis place don't look so bad," he said as he walked toward the crowded bar. "Let's start with a drink," he added, over his shoulder, bee-lining toward the only empty table. As I made my way after him I heard "Tears for Fears" on the jukebox—". . . nothing ever lasts forever. . . ." Ian and I had loved that song.

Ian. I'd often come here with him, something I'd neglected to remember in choosing this place. What had I been thinking?

I stubbed my toe on a bar stool occupied by a burly man. "Hey, watch where you're going!" he yelled. I apologized and moved toward Sal, who had already seated himself at the small square table covered with butcher paper. He waved me over. By the time I made it to him he had grabbed the waitress. He ordered a Long Island iced tea. "What'll the lady have?" he asked. I ordered a large margarita on the rocks, with salt.

"Dat sure is a Cali drink," he said, launching into why he could never live in "Cali." I tried to focus on what he was saying—"too sunny," "people are dumb"—but was distracted when he ripped off a piece of butcher paper, spit his gum into it, wadded it up, and threw it on the floor.

I stared at the wad. This scenario might have stumped even Commander Unander.

Our drinks arrived. "Thanks, Baby," Sal said to the cowboy-booted waitress. "I'll start a tab."

While I was wondering if I'd really just heard him call the waitress "baby," he dove into his Long Island iced tea without a word. "Oh. . . . Cheers!" I said, taking a gulp of my margarita before asking Sal about himself.

"I work at a bank—a branch out on the Island." He cradled his Island iced tea in both hands, leaned back in the small wooden chair, and went on to tell me about his media center; his car; his home; his monkey suits. I watched a bit of his drink leak out of the corner of his mouth.

"So," he asked, "how much they pay a fax-checker?"

"Fact-checker."

"Yeah. How much?"

I paused.

"What's wrong? You don't wanna tell me?"

"I'm sorry," I said, explaining that he'd caught me off guard—that before moving to New York I'd lived in London, where people didn't discuss such things.

"But you're in New York now, baby," he reminded me, informing me of his "gross annual income."

He was right. I was in New York. I was single, and I was on a date. So, I gamely told him my publishing-low salary, which evoked a "whoa" of disbelief.

I then launched into what I thought was a charming fact-checking anecdote about Jackie, who manned the trademark hotline phone. He interrupted me to discuss his "potential for growth" at the bank.

I hadn't even finished my first drink and I was feeling a strong urge to leave. I looked over at the bar and recalled a time Ian and I had gotten drunk on margaritas there. He'd leaned close and whispered in my ear. We could sit next to each other for hours, deeply enjoying each other's company, not having to say a word.

But he was off somewhere with his Spanish virgin, making wedding plans, no doubt, and I deserved another shot at love.

Determined to find common ground, I asked Sal if he had a favorite movie?

"*Goodfellas*—what a fuckin' fantastic movie! Didn't you love it?"

"I'm afraid I'm not a fan of gangster movies. I find them unsettling."

"Really? That's sorta weird." He took another swig of his Long Island iced tea, his eyes straying toward a tall blonde at the bar.

"I know. It is."

"But of course you've seen *The Godfather.*"

"I haven't."

He gasped, audibly. "You kiddin' me."

I tried sharing my childhood dread of having to see the severed head of my favorite animal in bed with someone but he wasn't listening.

"Jesus! That's fuckin' unbelievable! I can't even imagine that! I mean, you know, I know a lot a people who are involved with the Family. Where I grew up, they're everywhere."

"Wow," I said.

Sal finished his drink and shouted across the room: "Hey, baby—another!" I desperately wanted another too, but couldn't bring myself to copy his loud vibrato.

After a few minutes of staring at the gum/butcher's paper wad on the floor while Sal gave me a running commentary on the waitress's progress with his drink, I leapt in with another topic: family—not The Family, just his own.

"Let me tell you about my brother," he said. "Tony. He's a *loser.* Lives out in Montana, where there's nothin' but mountains."

I said nothing. He took my silence as approval.

"He's gettin' some stupid master's degree in *poetry*," he said, disdainfully.

"Really?" I asked, interested.

"Yeah. I keep tellin' him, 'you gotta get an MBA if you wanna do anythin' useful.' But no, he just hangs out in the mountains and writes poetry. He doesn't know the importance of doing an honest job—something not all artsy fartsy."

I wondered why I wasn't on a date with Tony. What was I doing? As much as I wanted this to work, I had to face the facts. I was on a date with the world's most incompatible guy for me. I didn't do well with businessmen; the mob gave me the creeps; I was partial to manners after all, and to parsable sentences. I wanted to discuss light and form and hang out in the mountains and write poetry.

I looked at my watch. "Oh, no," I said, "I have to go."

"Oh, uh, all right," Sal said. "I'm not really hungry either." He chugged the rest of his drink, then stood up and yelled for the waitress. "Yo, Sweetheart!"

"This is on me," he said, signing the bill. "You sure can't afford it."

He walked me home. I must have done a good job of hiding my inner monologue, because he was speaking of our next date, "I'll be sure not to wear my monkey suit," he emphasized.

I wish I could say I was mature enough to tell him I didn't think we were a likely match. Instead, the moment we got to my building I quickly thanked him and rushed through the front door before he could say—or do—anything. I went upstairs to my apartment, to the room I'd put together with furniture I'd found on the street or bought on the cheap.

I sat on my futon and thought about Ian, wondering if I'd ever be able to fall in love again. I thought about my mother, and how she'd tried to make everything okay. I felt so far from home.

I know it was wrong—and that Commander Unander and my mother would have disapproved—but for the next few weeks I had Rachel answer my calls and, if it were Sal, to say I wasn't available ("But nicely," I urged).

When my mother phoned, I tried to make light of the date by entertaining her. I focused on the wad of gum. "No!" she gasped. "He threw it on the floor?! He sounded so nice!" She laughed. "We'll that's the last time I'll ever try that."

And it was.

In time, I did come to feel at home in my apartment and in this city. I did go on many more dates—some with guys who even my mother thought were conceivably deserving of those linen hand towels from Ireland. And, eventually, I did manage to find love again, on my own, with my mother looking on in wonder.

The Marrying Man

Shari Goldhagen

My mother will tell anyone who'll listen about her daughter, the writer who lives in New York: other women getting their hair done in the upscale suburban Cincinnati salon; FedEx employees, when she's shipping me random packages of power bars, magazines, and spa gift certificates; and just about every person in any type of line—stand next to her and in thirty seconds you'll know all about how I had a book come out last spring and how I used to stalk celebrities for the *National Enquirer*. That's how I met Jeff three years ago—because my mother was in line for a Diet Coke during intermission at a matinee.

My parents were in town because my father had to work a trade show, so I took my mother to *Wonderful Town* on Broadway. It was about a girl from Ohio who moves to New York, gets a scary-ass apartment, goes on lots of dates, and tries to make it as a writer. It was pretty much the premise of my life, only with more musical numbers and jazz hands. This is what my mother apparently started telling everyone in the refreshment line during the break while I was downstairs in the ladies' room.

By the time we met up in our seats, my mother was flushed as if someone had spiked her Diet Coke with hard liquor.

"So I just talked to the nicest man, and I told him about you." She was trying to get all the info out before the curtain came up. "He works in media, too, so I gave him your number. But I think he'll probably want to date you. I showed him your picture."

"What?" The house lights were flickering, indicating the second act was eminent. I was yelling in a stage whisper, "You can't just give out that information."

"Because that's something you would never do?"

I got what she was saying. After breaking up with my high school/college/grad school sweetheart eighteen months before, I'd moved to New York from the Midwest. Single for the first time in my adult life, I'd been dating . . . a lot. I met men at coffeeshops, on the subway, at art openings, at readings, in bars, and walking down the street. I had business cards from every law firm/IBank/hedgefund in Manhattan, and after the fourth weekend in a row with a different guy at Nobu, the novelty of $25 edamame had worn off. And yet nothing had clicked. There was no spark to catch fire, and at the end of the night (or sometimes the next morning) we were just two sticks rubbing together.

The fact that my mother had met this man while I was in the bathroom in tourist-y Times Square wasn't necessarily promising, but really, how much worse could it be than the guy who picked me up while I was buying Monistat at Duane Reade?

"He probably won't even call," I said.

But call he did, the very next morning.

I was pleasantly surprised that the conversation about where we lived and what we did was relatively painless. Still I was skeptical.

"Come on, I already know your life story from the play," he joked. "And your mom wants us to go out. I think you should listen to her; she *is* your mother." The owner of a lifestyle media company, he said he had to attend a couple of shows the next day for Fashion Week—Marc Jacobs, Roberto Cavalli—names that were familiar in an abstract, other-half kind of way. "Maybe we can check those out and then go out to dinner?"

It was intimidating and exciting, and promised to be different from the dinners and drinks I'd been experiencing over the past months. I have to admit it was making me rethink my mother's other dismissed suggestions about such things as lipstick choices and necklines.

We agreed to meet at the Starbucks across the street from Bryant Park. When I started to explain what I looked like he said, "Don't bother. Your mother showed me your picture. I know you're adorable."

It was a promising start.

True to his word, Jeff knew me right away. The minute I walked into the crowded coffeeshop, he stood up and extended a hand. "You must be Shari," he said.

It was easy to tell why my mother liked him; to be honest, I didn't have too many problems with his looks myself. He was handsome; wavy black hair, strong features, and stylish wire-framed glasses. As would be expected, he was a good dresser in an understated, dark sweater and jeans way.

The conversation and the coffee went well. We were joking before the beverages cooled, and he was wonderfully attentive— pulling out my chair for me, asking follow-up questions, looking at my eyes and not my boobs. My mother was starting to look like the MVP of matchmaking.

We walked across the street to the tents set up in Bryant Park, and as promised, Jeff was on all kinds of lists. He'd mention his name and velvet ropes parted, reserved signs removed from seats. It was a little scary. I wasn't wearing Prada, but if Lauren Wiesenberger's bestseller was to be believed, the editor two seats down from us most definitely was. But Jeff made jokes to put me at ease, showing me he knew how silly the whole thing was.

"Now who would actually wear that?" he whispered into my ear as a model walked the runway in a feathered concoction. "It looks like a comforter exploded."

I giggled and soon we were talking about our favorite movies and confessing which of the classics we'd never read. The conversation took us to the next show without either one of us learning a thing about the coming year's hemlines.

"How old are you?" he asked, midway through the second show.

I was twenty-six at the time and saw no real reason to lie, so I didn't. But when I inquired about his age, he got quiet and looked away.

"Oh come on, if we go out again it will come up. Don't make me do a public records search on you."

"Okay, I just turned fifty." His eyes drifted down at his shoes—nice shoes I noticed, hip shoes—the kind of shoes that my father, who was only seven years older than Jeff, would never think to wear. "Does that bother you?"

The truth was, it didn't. I was surprised because he did look younger, and perhaps my mother wouldn't have been so quick to dole out my digits had she known the guy had passed the half-century mark, but really it didn't make that much difference. Heck, he might not have even been the oldest guy I'd dated—a lot of time I didn't care enough to ask.

"It's not a dealbreaker," I said, and smiled. Still, Jeff looked downtrodden so I reached for his hand and dug into my guts for my throaty/sexy voice. "Although my grandmother did tell me never to trust a man who wasn't married by forty-five."

This was in fact true. My father's mother had been married five times and had all kinds of rules that seemed ripped from some sort of kitschy retro book you see on the tables at Urban Outfitters. Still I was hoping that throaty/sexy and the hand-holding would be enough to get the date back on track.

A concerned V wrinkled his brow.

"Oh, I plan to propose to someone in the next six months," he said. "And I'll be married by the end of the year."

I'd been in NYC for less than two years, but it was plenty of time for me to know this was not typical language from a Big Apple Bachelor. What was especially interesting was that one of the models was walking down the runway in an outfit that clearly exposed one breast, and Jeff didn't even notice.

"Really?"

"Yes," he said. "I've worked my whole life to make money, and now it's time that I enjoy it with someone special."

"Good to know," I said, hoping that would be the end of the matrimony portion of the evening.

Around us the show was ending. Magazine editrixes were gathering $6,000 handbags and pocket puppies; frazzled assistants were on the move with cell phones balanced between their ears and shoulders, schedules and clipboards in hand. Jeff suggested we stop by his co-op on 57th street and decide on dinner.

If his apartment was an example of how he planned to "enjoy" his life, I was game. The decadent, sprawling three-bedroom boasted floor-to-ceiling windows with remote control–operated blinds, lots of marble and granite, and a fabulous view of the Chrysler Building. There were paintings on the wall by artists I'd read about—Francine Tint, Terry Winters, and some rich-colored swirly thing that may have been a real Kandinsky. There was a shimmering black grand piano; my apartment didn't have a drawer in the kitchen.

"Wait until you see my place in East Hampton," he responded when I mentioned how gorgeous his home was. "And the boat."

But I couldn't fully enjoy the tour because of the commentary that went with it. When he showed me a work area in the den, he mentioned that if we were to get married I could write there. One of the extra bedrooms could be for our baby, if I was inter-ested in having children—it would totally be "my call." He'd give me the walk-in closet, because his stuff fit in the smaller one.

I wanted to go back to chatting about our favorite movies and how no one we'd ever met had actually read *War and Peace*.

"I want to show you something," he said, disappearing into another room.

He returned a few minutes later with something held between his thumb and forefinger. As he got closer, it became apparent that this something was a two-carat emerald-cut engagement ring in a platinum setting.

"I just wanted to show you how serious about this I am," he said, explaining that the ring was his grandmother's and he'd brought it back on his last trip home. "I just wanted to be ready when I meet the right person, which just might be you."

I was a struggling writer pouring wine for ten bucks an hour at Wine and Spirits and doing some odd telemarketing job that involved calling doctors' offices. Making the rent on my sixth-floor walk-up every month was an epic stretch.

And here was Jeff standing in front of me with a diamond ring that I could probably trade in for a car, offering me a way out and a key to a three-bedroom two minutes from the Park.

It wasn't a proposal, I don't think. He was slouching a little, but he wasn't kneeling, and while his voice might have risen slightly at the end of the sentence, it really wasn't a question. But it was clearly getting close. The ring was big, but it seemed to be taking up the entire apartment. Literally, it was the only thing I could focus on.

I'd be lying if I didn't say that a part of me was tempted. Somewhere, I'd read that arranged marriages have the same success rates as love marriages. And we weren't complete strangers, we'd known each other for nearly two-and-a-half hours. So far we appeared to have many similar interests. I liked the finer things, and he had them.

But it was more than just his really cool stuff that gave me pause.

My heart had been bludgeoned when the high school/college/grad school sweetheart and I parted. We'd dated for seven years and broke up because he didn't want to marry me. And here was someone who, having known me for all of 153 minutes, was offering what my ex hadn't—a life and a future with all the trimmings. It would be the end to all the games: The bad dates where, midway between the appetizer and the entrée, I'd seriously contemplate crawling out the ladies' room window; those nights of waiting by the phone for someone to call. Then another thought occurred to me: *He probably only has another twenty years left—I could still have a life after him.*

That's the moment I knew I had to get out of that apartment and away from Jeff. So I invented a family emergency/a freelance assignment that needed to be finished/dog that needed to be walked/hair that needed to be washed/Monistat that needed to be purchased. I have no memory of what I said or how I got out of the apartment. All I know is a few minutes later I was rummaging through the bottom of my purse for subway fare back to the Lower East Side. By the time he called later that night I was eating tuna fish from a can on the worn futon I'd been dragging around since college. Still I didn't answer the phone.

My mother's not allowed to give out my phone number anymore. But I've often wondered about Jeff since that night—not about what we could have had, but whether he did in fact propose to someone within his allotted six months. My guess is that he had no problem finding a taker. It was a *really* nice apartment.

You're a Writer, She's a Writer!

Rebecca Bloom

When you're thirty and still single, everyone has someone for you. All of a sudden you enter into this new territory where you're an extremely eligible piece of meat. Career, check. Friends, check. Modern collectible furniture with that ideal *Domino* magazine spin, check. Total independence, check.

You're the marrying kind now. The woman who can manage a bank account in one hand while cooking a gourmet dinner sans cook book with the other, as an iPod—stocked with music that reviewers for *Rolling Stone* would approve of—plays in the background. No longer the young twenty-something discovering yourself through a series of misadventures that you conveniently no longer see as earth shattering regrets, just-hand-slapping-the-forehead, why-did-I-do-that regrettables.

One would think a mother who's lived through my dating habits, and even read about them in my first novel, which, though fictional, did divulge my romantic entanglements and types, would know what floats her daughter's boat no matter how old she gets. That I will never ignore the hot guy in the vintage car especially if he has the right hair, a guitar, and a battered copy of Camus in his back seat. She should have catalogued in her brain all the hopelessly romantic defining details that compose *the* guy for her daughter. But, my mother never gets it right, and somehow forgets the real girl behind all the grown up accoutrements I have begun to amass.

There are things you can tell just by looking at my mother. She's got impeccable style that's all her own. She knows her Bendel's from her Bergdorf's, her Spy bags from her Speedys. While I used to cringe at her artfully deconstructed Comme des Garçons outfits as a young girl, now, I admire her personal vision, and those bags are quite easily stashed under the arm and "borrowed." You can also tell she's a glass-half-full kind of person. Smile lines tug at her face, a face free from that typical L.A. botox glaze. But, alas, my hip, trendy, smart mother should never put matchmaker on her long list of achievements.

When my mother suggested her first meet and greet with a son of a very distant friend, I was twenty, home from college for winter break and in my alternative/artsy/pothead phase. I liked the guys at Brown with longish hair, the perfectly rumpled flannel shirts that I snuck out of their rooms carefully beneath my winter J.Crew pea coats. The guys that taught me how to take a bong hit, roll a joint, and put on a condom.

I primped, preened, and went, unwillingly but ever dutifully. Fake IDs at the ready, we met at a local bar, and I stood face to face with a clean-cut, tucked in, khaki-wearing, all-American football player who then proceeded to chug beer all night while regaling me with lengthy stories of keg stands and pub crawls that ended with mornings getting legs and eggs at the local collegiate strip club. He got blurrier and blurrier and I got more and more bored.

The next date occurred about two years later when I was still caught up in the flush of a crush on a completely unavailable rapper/law student with a strong face, curly black hair, and the ability to make me swoon like a puppy eyeing a bone across a crowded pet store. We had had the "we have to be friends talk" weeks before but I just couldn't shake his sway, so I said yes to my eager mother knowing this was her way of trying to band-aid my broken heart.

The set up picked me up. He wasn't half bad. Good jeans, button-down shirt, and slightly wrinkled blazer. We went to dinner, he was quiet. We went for coffee, he was still quiet. We went for drinks, he was too quiet. A marathon date with a man that offered monosyllabic answers to any question I asked could easily be given an honorable mention under the definition of torture in the dictionary. To top it off, silent guy eyed a few other guys at the club we ended up at.

Two strikes and I'm out. I'd had enough. No more was my mother to be wooed by her lady friends and their eloquent tales of their sons/cousins/friends of friends. She was to reject any possibility, keep her mind on anything and everything else, and let me find my own way through the tumultuous sea of imperfect suitors. That was until she had a lightbulb moment reading the *Jewish Journal*. Somehow in those printed pages, she was convinced she met my dream man. Unfortunately, she didn't tell me until her plan was already set in motion and it was too late to break the bulb and shatter her illusions.

There was no profile whereby all his stats were laid out on the page. You know, the important things like what he looked like, his age, what he looked like, where he came from, and what he looked like. There wasn't even a fuzzy picture on a contributors page for her to reference. No, this man was pen without a face, a new columnist for the journal.

Without consulting me, my mother wrote him the following e-mail:

"Dear Matt, I have never done anything like this before, and I am sure my daughter is going to kill me for it later, but I had to write. While reading your thoughts about L.A. and dating and figuring out how to live in this crazy town, I thought about my daughter, Rebecca. I think that the two of you would really get along. She, too, is a writer. A successful novelist, her first book, *Girl Anatomy*, was just released in paperback. She writes about the same sort of things from a woman's perspective. I think you would love her. Again, I never do this, but I think you and she would really hit it off. How strange is this? Best, Ruth."

My mother knew she'd crossed some unfamiliar line, and kept all of this on the DL. I guess something about pimping her daughter out online to a random journalist gave her pause. And, only after I received the oddest e-mail from said man, was her plot revealed. Not only had she been e-mailing him once a day for a week or so, baiting him into a sense of familiarity, she gave him my e-mail freely and for all intents and purposes, told him to e-mail me and ask me on a date. There was this odd man who knew things about me, what I did, what I wrote, where I went to school, and the area I lived in. It was unnerving.

Matt wrote that my mother had sent him my info because she thought we would be a good match. He prefaced with some plucky comment on feeling strange to e-mail a stranger by way of her mother who he doesn't know from Adam and wouldn't it be funny if we actually liked each other.

Only after cursing my mother on the phone and demanding every e-mail she sent Matt so I could at least get a feel for what she had divulged, and a few of my own witty e-mail exchanges with him, did I decide to meet him. What if this was my story?

We made a date online; I picked a spot, a bar famous for its outdoor patio, beer on tap, and fish-and-chip crowd. I got dressed carefully, trying to create that ideal offhand outfit that was datey without being slutty, feminine without looking like I had tried too hard. I chose my date dress, a light blue BCBG dress with a paisley pattern that had gotten me through a fair number of firsts without any major wardrobe malfunctions. I parked, walked up to the bar, saw this little guy in khakis, a blue button down, and a cell phone belt keeping time with his foot in front, and I instantly knew that this nebbishy man was Matt. I'm not a heightest or anything but I do have to date above my bra strap. A guy who you tower over in flats just isn't going to work. But I smiled, and made my introduction:

"Hi." I said, walking toward him. "Matt?"

"Yeah, Rebecca?" He offered me a clammy hand.

"That's me." Shaking. "Nice to meet you. Shall we?" I said, trying to move things along.

"Well, we have a little problem. Seems like they are closed for a private party."

"Okay, well . . . we can try Les Deux? It's around the corner. You can follow me."

"Great, but let's go together. Why waste money to park two cars?"

And he's cheap.

"I saw you park right there, let's take your car." He started walking toward my ride with me reluctantly following him. Somehow, not a minute later we were sitting side by side, with him in my personal space.

At the next restaurant we sat at a table outside and when the waitress came by I ordered a glass of wine. He opted for sparkling water.

"I don't drink," he stated.

"Ever?"

"Never. Have never even had a sip of Manashevitz. Just never had the desire."

"Even in college? Not one rowdy evening with your friends?" I was shocked.

"Nope. All that drunken tomfoolery seemed a bit childish."

Tomfoolery? Who says that? I tried to change subjects, talking about how funny it was that my mother had set us up. Then we shared first date crap, what do you do, I just moved here, L.A. is so crazy, and after about twenty minutes and him proceeding to bring up his Orthodox parents and how strict they were, I started glazing over.

"My parents think I'm so wild for even living in L.A. They think L.A. is this hotbed of secularism."

"Why did you come out here?"

"To get away really, and I got offered a good job I didn't want to pass up. Living in L.A. is my version of rebelling."

"Ah, I see. Move to the place of sinners, movie stars, and bad E! *True Hollywood Stories* to test out your wild streak."

"I guess I am just 'a wild and crazy guy.'" Then he did an imitation of Steve Martin from *Saturday Night Live*. "Get it? *SNL?*"

"Sure, yeah. I love Steve Martin. So, do you like it here? Seems from what you write about that you're having fun checking out this city."

"Sure, its fine."

"Favorite spots?"

"Love the Getty, and I have actually been spending my free time at that great library downtown."

"I don't think I've ever been."

By now I couldn't look past his bald spot from years spent with yarmulke on his head, nor could I ignore the fact that in these twenty minutes he had not taken a breath! If my previous fix up failed to utter a sound, this guy couldn't get over the tonality of his own voice. He talked and talked and talked until I was convinced he could power Utah with the energy created by the output of his own breath. My wine went down fast and I signaled to the waitress for another.

"Really? The library is so cool, we should go. They have all these great old texts, really gets you going as a writer."

I smiled, nodded and wiped nonchalantly at my brow trying to remove the lovely spray of spit Matt projected at me. Then, as if it couldn't get worse, I heard someone call *my* name. I turned around to find my ex—looking fantastic in a Paul Smith button down I had bought him in Paris—and his new perky blonde girlfriend smiling down at me. Delightful. As blondie played with her perfect hair and adjusted the strap on the tight cotton tank-top that was accentuating her voluptuous assets and asserting her buxom power, I wished I was a super hero with any or all the following superhuman powers: invisibility, time travel, or image morphing. I wanted to disappear, pretend like the evening never happened, or change my date into George Clooney with a snap of my fingers.

I made introductions and Matt invited them to sit with us. The blonde made the face I was thinking in my head and my ex darted away like the reptile he was. Matt sat back down and without missing a beat in his monologue continued spewing about nothing. I flagged down the waitress and ordered another round.

Numbed by cheap wine and boring conversation, I sat there wishing my mother had never started this little adventure of hers into my love life. I paid for my wine—he didn't even offer, which while I know he had water, would have been a nice gesture.

Back in my car, I turned the radio on loudly hoping it would drown him out. Unfortunately, he talked louder. I pulled over at his car and hoped he'd hop out.

Not a chance. He lingered. Talked. Lingered and talked more. And I realized he'd yet to ask me anything about myself. I watched the clock radio tick on, his droning becoming background noise that I thought I could almost ignore if it weren't for the random spit that kept landing on my cheek.

Finally, he went in for a kiss. I turned away, and he hit my hair. He laughed and tried again to the same effect. I reached over, opened the door for him. Enough was enough.

I called my mom the next morning and exiled her from my love land. After listening to my take of a date gone wrong, I think she finally got the message that meddling was never a good idea. She vowed, again, to keep her nose out of my business. And, this time, I'm sure she'll listen—for at least a year or so.

The School Teacher Who Couldn't Commit

Adina Kay

I should have known never to date a Hebrew School teacher. But when you're single, you lose perspective. So when my mother said she'd met a guy and thought he might be my type, I said, "tell me more."

My mother's funny. When she asks me questions about dating, her face loses its lines and goes completely young. Talking about boys keeps her entertained for hours. Her eyebrows raise, her nose and cheeks flush pink. She giggles. She speaks to me so tentatively I feel badly, knowing her caution is in response to my potential to go loose-cannon on her.

On this night, she mustered courage and pounced.

"So, Dee, anyone new in your classes?" she bravely posited.

"What do you *mean*, Mom? It's the middle of the semester! No one's new. My grad program is full of self-interested, latently homosexual, untalented waifs who think their every fart—let alone their novel—is special." (You see why she tiptoed around me.)

"I was interviewing new teachers at Eastern Synagogue today," she continued. "And I met this one guy, Danny, and he seems great. I think he's your type—not too Jewy at all! "I mean, he's no Don Juan, honey, but he's very nice looking." She added this last part to cover her bases. In case I was expecting an actual Don Juan.

Our first date was at a bar near Union Square. I suggested the locale, halfway between my Upper West Side apartment, and Danny's, in Brooklyn.

The date started out well. Entering a bar to meet a blind date is undeniably nerve wracking. All around, couples who had likely met in a more organic fashion leaned in close over glasses of Petite Syrah. I wished I was them. But when I got to the back of the restaurant and spotted him—the one guy sitting alone—I slapped my mother a mental high-five. This guy *was* cute! Floppy brown hair, big eyes, a wide smile. I approached. The cute man with a sprinkle of freckles on his nose got up to greet me. He was polite! And tall! A tall polite Jew! It was a winter miracle.

"It's nice to meet you," Danny bellowed. Oh joy! A deep voice! This Adonis must have had some non-Jewish blood in him; he was perfectly male!

Three drinks, two hours and some not-bad conversation later, Danny walked me to the subway. My head buzzed with the promise of a first kiss. I walked close to Danny, bumping into him until he finally grabbed my hand.

We descended into the subway station and stopped talking. My cheeks reddened. Against the foul tiled walls of the 4,5,6 station, we kissed. I had to stand on my toes to reach him. The kiss was soft but Danny was serious. He kept his eyes shut tight and punctuated the long, soulful kiss (open mouthed, his fairly large but not unseemly lips covered my own smaller mouth) with three or four short soft kisses on the lips. My cheeks felt hot. I pulled away and looked down. Danny touched my chin, like an old man might do. We promised each other a second date, and I floated home on a cloud of vanilla vodka and butterflies.

Mother Cupid had done good. I couldn't believe it.

One week later, Danny met me in my neighborhood. I was relieved when I saw him; he was still cute, wearing a blue shirt untucked and khaki pants. His shoes were passable: no buckles. Plain black loafers. *Phew.*

We ate Chinese food and saw an early movie. I can't remember a word of what we talked about at dinner. All I could think about was kissing him again. And the fact that as he walked through the crowded restaurant, all the women turned to stare.

We went to my apartment. One thing led to another. We moved from the couch to my bedroom in record time. Danny's shirt came off. Lovely pecs! And hairless! A tall, polite, hairless Jew! This couldn't be real. But alas, around his neck hung an absurdly large, gold Star of David. His cuteness factor dropped a bit when I saw it, but he said it was once his grandfather's, a Holocaust survivor.

Once he mentioned the Holocaust I knew I couldn't ask him to take it off, though it seemed like a safety hazard. But when one of the huge points struck me in the face, Danny removed it. Moments later our noses collided, another awkward fumble. "The hazards of two Jews kissing," he said, chuckling.

But just as things got steamy, he jumped up, padded over to his backpack lying on the floor, and opened it. He fished out a binder containing Hebrew School plans and plopped it on my lap.

"I thought you could look over my lesson plans," he said, grinning goofily.

I laughed. "Yeah, right," I joked. "And then we can read the *Jewish Week* and study Torah."

Danny looked crestfallen. "No, really," he said. "My stuff is good. Could you just look it over?" He slipped the big Star back over his head and pulled on his shirt.

Reluctantly, I started reading about Danny's plans for a Chanukah trivia-bowl.

"Flip to the section on the origins of the dreidel," he asked. "Too simple for sixth graders? Be honest."

Honestly? I could care less about the pedagogic implications of infantilizing spoiled East Side rich kids by asking them to construct spinning tops out of play dough. Let them eat latkes! I looked at him, standing in the middle of my bedroom in his boxers; hair mussed, expression earnest, waiting for me to answer.

"Dan, this lesson plan is pitch-perfect for the thirteen-year-old set."

Danny grinned and sauntered over. With one swift gesture, he pushed his binder to the floor and climbed back into bed. Jewish-education-as-aphrodisiac. Who knew?

Moments later Danny whispered: "Do you want to have sex?"

"Um," I stuttered, "Yes. Do you have a condom?"

Was that a snort? I wasn't sure. It was dark. I couldn't see his face. He probably had the winter sniffles.

"Uh, no, I don't have one," he answered. He didn't sound regretful.

"That's okay," I said. "There's a Duane Reade up the block. Let's run over."

Danny was quiet. Then he said, "You know what? I'm really tired. In fact, I'm wiped out."

I couldn't believe this.

He wasn't done. "Also, Adina? I'm too big for condoms. They hurt when I try to fit them on."

Now it was my turn to snort with derision. But instead, I accepted this preposterousness and smiled in the dark. He was a phallic freak of nature. But he was mine.

One more week and one more date. This time I offered to go to Brooklyn. Oh happy day! Cute man's apartment awaits! Right? Wrong.

I took an obscurely lettered train and emerged in the quiet outer borough. Walking up Seventh Avenue I was struck by how few people were on the street. It felt lonely. Would Danny even miss me if I didn't show up? As quickly as the thought seized me, I pushed it away.

I found his brownstone. A dried out flower-bed was attached to a front window, and old gym shoes hung over the electric wires crisscrossing the street. The light surrounding his block was grey. I knocked at Danny's apartment door and heard his muffled shout from inside: The door was open, I should come on in. Gone, I guess, were the days of him getting up to greet me.

As I entered, I heard the plinky notes of a cartoon soundtrack and saw the glare of the television. A blue light fell upon the room. Strewn about were the telltale signs of a man-boy. Wires attached to video games and movie-watching mechanisms, joysticks, empty take-out boxes. Danny was sprawled on the couch, surrounded by balled up tissues. It smelled like feet and fried rice.

So . . . bachelor pads shock the aesthetic senses at first. Still essentially amused, I asked to see his room. Danny turned to me slowly, keeping one eye on the TV.

"Uh, I'd rather you not go in there," he said.

Such a joker! Now there was the funny guy I remembered from our first date!

"Hilarious, Danny. Really, come on, lazybones! Get up! Let me see your room!"

"Seriously Adina. It's not ready for you to see. Stop asking."

My mouth dropped open. "Not ready for me? What the heck does that mean?" I stuttered.

"Oh come on," he snapped. "It doesn't mean anything. I just would rather you not go in there."

My head filled with Technicolor images of Danny's bedroom, littered with crack-cocaine vials, an illicit cadre of kiddie-porn, or a secret wife chained to the bed.

Just then, he stretched his arm out from the couch and waved me over, narrowing his eyes into a come-hither stare. You might not believe me, but the look was enough to make me forget, at least for the moment, the absurdity of not being allowed into his bedroom. Danny pulled me on to the couch and into a tight embrace. He kissed my neck and asked if I wanted to order pizza. I rallied, quelling the voices in my head that were protesting against this all. I wanted pizza. I wanted to stay.

After hours on the couch, we'd watched every sitcom on Nick at Night, plus played a round of his favorite videogame. It was 1:00 A.M. I asked him if he wanted to wash up and get ready for bed. I was eager to snuggle on a larger surface than the scratchy woolen couch.

Danny tugged his arm out from underneath me and furrowed his brow. "Oh, see, I don't think you should stay here tonight," he said, looking away.

"Wait, you don't want me to stay here? Why? Because of your *bedroom*, Danny? Is this for real?" Let him get angry at my tone,

I thought, already calculating how much a cab would cost to get home.

"No, it's *not* the bedroom, Adina," Danny mimicked, making his voice high and whiney, apparently imitating mine. "Not every date has to end in a sleepover, you know."

This *was* about the bedroom, but I was out of words. How do you beg your boyfriend let you see his bedroom?

Later, as I sat in the backseat of the taxi cab I'd hailed, alone, (he didn't walk me to the door or to the street to find a cab), I seethed. I hated Danny just then. As the cab rattled over the bridge and back to the land of adults who see each others' bedrooms, I decided I wouldn't keep seeing Danny if the ridiculousness continued. Then I changed my mind. Who was I kidding? He was cute, and let's just say it: I was desperate.

One week later I was on the F train to Brooklyn, again. It seemed Danny didn't like coming uptown, and anything past Union Square qualified as uptown. Still, I was hopeful: He'd promised this time we'd eat out. That would mean we'd *go* out!

When I got to his place he was dressed. His hair was wet. He had showered. He had stood up! He looked great. But alas, right away, he asked if we could "rest" before dinner. Apparently he'd spent the afternoon chasing kids in the courtyard outside Hebrew school. They were playing tag. He had been "it."

We plopped down on the scratchy couch. I watched his pants wrinkle. When he kicked off his shoes, I knew we weren't going anywhere, ever. Sure enough, moments later Danny looked over and told me that on second thought, he wasn't up for dinner out. For old time's sake, I asked if he might want to go rest on his bed, like civilized people. He groaned and told me to quit asking about the bedroom. I took one last look at his adorable face and his fit body, now splayed on the couch like a beached Abercrombie model, and decided it was done. "Goodbye," I said, making my way toward the front door. "You are so lazy you make me tired."

The door clicked shut behind me and I stood alone on Danny's front stoop. It was dark and quiet on the street. It was late. A cab—that most precious vision in late-night Brooklyn—passed by and honked its horn. I didn't want a ride, though. I didn't want to sit down. Unlike Danny, at the ripe old age of 28 I still had some energy left in me. I wanted to walk, and breathe, and live. My mother, thankfully, never fixed me up again.

Orange You Glad
I Didn't Say Banana?

Molly Prather

My mom, like most people, hated her job. She worked in a misery of a law office she called "her living nightmare," referred to her fellow paralegals as "harpies," and named the boss's wife "Satan Bitch." Despite the black cloud she endured nine to five, five days a week, there was a brief time when the clouds parted and the sun shone brightly. It was the day Todd, a younger brother of one of the lawyers down the hall, was hired.

Todd, a cross between Goofy and Chandler Bing, aged twenty-eight, and my mother, a cross between Annie Hall and Nancy Drew, aged forty-eight, became fast friends. They quickly found a routine of inside jokes, conspiratorial chats, and water cooler gossip that I imagined to be somewhere along the lines of:

"Oh, Todd. Your Elmer Fudd impersonation is incredibly realistic. You *must* have a girlfriend."

"No. Why?"

"I find that hard to believe."

"Well, if you know someone, set me up."

So she did. With me.

Informing me that I'd been fixed up with Todd, who happened to be heir to a sizeable family fortune, Mom failed to mention a few things. First, Todd shook hands like a fish. A man with little to no handshake is, as far as I'm concerned, not a man at all. Limp in the hand category is analogous with similarly listless body parts and will never result in my being thrown up against a wall, nor ever grabbed by my hair just right—close to the scalp, right above the neck—in a fit of mind-blowing passion.

Second, he was almost thirty and living with his parents in what turned out to be a navy blue, baseball-wallpapered room with an alarming amount of decorative sports paraphernalia that would cause an eleven-year-old to squeal with delight.

And the third thing Mom forgot to mention: He had an incredibly specific idea of what was funny.

Now, there are a million and a half reasons mother/daughter matchmaking should have been prohibited in our family. First and foremost, that as a feral middle-aged woman approaching menopause, my mother's judgment was impaired from one too many screenings of *The Graduate*. But, more significantly, my mother and I have the same taste in absolutely nothing. She loves to wear primary colored socks and homemade jewelry; I'm rarely seen in anything other than black and silver hoop earrings. She's an avid fan of Anne Rice, listens to Neil Diamond without a trace of irony, and enjoys the fellowship of enthusiastic Christian housewives. I read the *New Yorker*, listen to Jeff Buckley, even when it's nice outside, and go to independent films alone. Why on earth would I like someone she picked out for me?

Allowing myself the, "What would it be like to marry into a family that owns large parts of Orange County?" Cinderella fantasy, I agreed to go out with Todd.

On our first date, I was running late. Todd, on the other hand, was not and thought it proper to show up thirty-five minutes early. My mother answered the door, ensuring me a few extra minutes as the sun has both risen and set in the time my mother has spent chatting up prior gentlemen callers. Blowing out my hair, squirming into a dress and heels for the first time in months, I put some finishing touches on my White Knight daydream: Me, the struggling musical theater artist relieved of finishing my degree at a state university by the Orange County aristocrat who, with his dashing wit and impeccable taste, would introduce me to a Southern California I had never known. When I finally waltzed downstairs forty-five minutes later, I was rendered speechless—and not in a Kay Jewelers commercial way. It was more of an "Oh my God, you're wearing a tracksuit" way.

Todd stood 6'3" in his spanking white Asics running shoes, an uneven grin, a mess of sandy locks, and the lack of musculature akin to a fifty-year-old man. In an extended attempt to downplay his fortune—I hoped—he wore a nylon tracksuit comparable to those that overweight, middle-age, suburban dads wear to coach their daughter's junior high basketball team. It wasn't even the high-end, sexy type that Diddy and Jay-Z sport for autograph signings at Virgin Megastores.

"Circle gets the square!" exclaimed my knight.

"What the hell is he talking about?" I thought to myself.

"Your chariot awaits, m'lady," grandly gesturing toward his Honda.

"Is he serious?" thinks me-self.

His Kermit green, yellow accented suit made a haunting "swish-swish" sound reminiscent of a fleshy woman walking in control top pantyhose as he followed me out to his car. The silent (save for Michael McDonald on his stereo) ride to dinner gave me time to reconfigure how the night was going to play out. Okay, maybe he wasn't attractive, well dressed, or hip to anything, but he was loaded and that should count for something, right? My foolish anticipation of a five-star dinner with Ritchie Rich left me sorely disappointed—and incredibly overdressed—when he pulled into the parking lot of BJ's Pizza.

As we approached the entrance of the restaurant, I crossed my fingers that his family owned the place or that he'd rented out the entire patio to cast his princely spell over me. When we sat down, it was not in an incredibly romantic reserved garden patio, nor in a candlelit, high-backed booth with a bottle of champagne chilling. Just a plain two-top at your basic suburbia eatery that could've doubled as a Cheesecake Factory, TGIF, Chili's, or some combination of the three.

Before the waitress had an opportunity to welcome us, Todd took an obvious glance at her nametag and was off and running.

"Aimie! I love that name! I love the name Aimie! I used to have a dog named Amy! And with an 'i-e'? Exotic. Well, Aimes, you're here to keep us right on target, so we'll just start out with the artichoke spinach dip, the fried cheese sticks, and the jalapeño poppers for an appetizer. Then we'll do the alfredo deep dish with extra sauce on the side for dinner, and go ahead and throw in two Pazookies for dessert."

Simultaneously with the waitress sprinting away to put in our order for all the food in the restaurant, Todd asked me if I knew why the suspenders were arrested.

"For holding up a pair a pants," he informed me as though I was the idiot.

Then he leaned in and put his hand behind my head. As I asked God, Jesus, and everyone else in heaven that they halt his public display of affection, he surprised us all by revealing the quarter that had been hiding in my ear. I had very mixed feelings about that quarter—it was both a relief and a sobering indication of where the night was headed. If I had wanted to go out with someone who pulls quarters out from behind people's ears I would have gone out with my grandpa. When I was eight.

As the endless plates of cheese and grease-laden food arrived at our table, Todd continued to assault the waitress and me with his *Mad Magazine* witticisms. Fortunately for the waitress, she was able to flee our table at the onslaught while I was left unarmed.

Todd leaned in again and spoke quietly, forcing me to get closer to him.

"Knock-knock."

You've got to be kidding me. "Who's there?"

"Norma Lee."

"Norma Lee who?"

"Normally I don't go around knocking on doors. Do you want to buy a set of encyclopedias?"

Normally, I don't contemplate suicide on first dates, but for you, Todd, I am making an exception.

"Knock-knock."

I took a deep breath. "Seriously?"

"Knock-knock."

"Todd, it's getting late. I have things in my life I need to get done at some point and should probably go now."

"Knock-knock."

"Todd, I really don't feel comfortable answering the door right now."

"I'm going to keep knocking until you answer."

"Believe me, I know."

"Knock-knock."

I hate my life. "Who's there?"

"Spank."

"Spank who?"

"Spank you."

"Don't even think about it."

"Knock-knock."

"Who's there?"

"Orange."

"Orange who?

"Orange you glad I came a knockin'?"

Truthfully, not at all.

Needless to say, there was no goodnight kiss, and Cinderella was home *way* before midnight.

Over the next few weeks, I suffered Todd's pizza fetish hoping at some point he'd break and reward me with a poached lobster dinner at the Summit House or a Tiffany's charm bracelet. I figured this all must be part of some carefully constructed evaluation to see if I could love Todd for Todd. I couldn't. I was sick of dating boys my own age who'd take me on "creative" dates because they were college broke. I wanted a rich boyfriend. But like the man who asked the genie for a Maserati and received a shiny car that wouldn't start, I forgot to ask the genie that my rich boyfriend be loaded *and* socially adept. Over the course of twenty-one days, I'd heard close to 9,000 knock-knock jokes, and I knew exactly what happened when a priest, a rabbi, and a blonde walked into a bar. He was all things opposite of what I find attractive—sheltered and predictably conservative, over-friendly with waitresses, a bad tipper, and blond. The type of guy born to vote Republican but the first to finance your abortion because his old-money, devoutly Catholic parents would kill him if he had a child out of wedlock.

While my disgust with Todd's warm-up attire, his penchant for heart attack inducing cuisine, and his visible saliva, increased daily, so did my mother's adoration for everything Todd.

"Todd did the most dead-on Daffy Duck impression in the office today that I have ever seen."

"Todd called me eleven times today asking if my refrigerator was running! I'd be lying if I said I didn't get up to check more than once to see if it was."

Listening to her beam about Todd's comedy travails, I didn't know whether to be horrified at him, her, or both.

"Knock-knock."

Definitely both.

"Who's there?"

Invasion of the Body Snatchers. Todd had gotten to my mother and washed her brain with a terrible sense of humor.

"Sally."

You know how people say you grow up to be just like you mother. . . .

"Sally, who?"

"Sally pledge of allegiance. No wait, Sadie. . . ."

I'm going to drive my car off the side of a cliff when this joke is over.

"Sadie—what are you talking about?"

"No, wait . . . I was supposed to say *Sadie*, so it would be "sadie pledge. . . ."

Key in ignition, destination cliff.

Oh my God. You don't retell bad jokes of boys with poor taste in everything from food to witticisms if you don't want to make out with them. Luckily for Todd, just as I was reaching the limit of my pizza and bad joke tolerance, he had finally found his audience. My mother.

I would come home from school, and he would be there with my mom drinking a bottle of Rosemount Shiraz, surfing joke Web sites, and eating a half pepperoni, half vegetarian pizza, "waiting to surprise me" when I got home. Curiously, by the time I arrived, neither pizza nor wine was leftover from my surprise dinner. On more than one occasion I walked in on Mom giggling and flirting at Todd's buffoonery in such a way that I knew precisely what was happening.

With the desire of bowing out of the situation as quickly and gracefully as possible, I broke things off with Todd. Amid our "it's not you, it's me" conversation, he did in fact give me a couple of ideas about why he believed the chicken had crossed the road. And, with a boldness not unlike him, asked if I minded if he asked out my friend Courtney. Mind? I would have called her in that instant myself if it guaranteed never having to see Todd again.

My mother, who'd turned into Fun Time Chatty Kathy anytime Todd's name came up in conversation, on the other hand, did mind. Having Todd at her, or her daughter's, arm's length was one thing; having him at someone else's was another thing entirely. Depending on the day, she would give me the silent treatment or yell hysterically at me for not emptying the dishwasher. Living at home with Desperate Housewife #6 got to the point of agony. There were no more inaccurate retellings of knock-knock jokes, no relaying of grade-school office pranks, no reenactments of Todd's *Looney Toon* impersonations. Clearly, as our house took on the air of a high school hallway with girls plotting revenge on the other for their own misery, there was no longer room for the two of us. One of us had to go and since the house was in my mother's name, I was out of luck.

The next day while Mom and Todd were at work—he warming her heart with atrocious knock-knock jokes, she encouraging him with her excessive giggling—I packed up my room and moved into Courtney's house.

Once I settled into Courtney's guest bedroom, I finally had a moment of, "What the fuck just happened?" Yes, my mom failed to learn the preeminent junior high lesson that you shouldn't set up your friend—or, in this case, your daughter—with the boy you are crushing on. But it was actually my astoundingly shallow materialism that got me kicked out of my childhood home. My mom fell for the real Todd—magic tricks, Catskill comedy, track suits—while I fell for the promise of fancy dinners and Tiffany jewelry. There is something truly wonderful about finding a person you feel so strongly toward that you'll do anything just to keep them close—even if it's completely frowned upon by the better part of society. So, it's hard to say which one of us had committed the greater transgression. At the end of the day, it was I who, when I heard the knock, should've looked through the keyhole, saw sun-reflecting Adidas pants, and not answered the door. Unfortunately, I hadn't heard the one about the girl getting set up by her mother on a date with a guy who shook hands like a fish.

Stranded

Tara Bahrampour

I lay on the icy slope, digging my fingers in to keep from sliding. Snow blew across my legs. My family had no idea where I was. Only this boy, my date, knew, and he had disappeared into the whiteness.

I hadn't exactly put myself in this situation. I could never have gotten a date on my own in the first place. Boys didn't talk to me. I was thirteen, with oily skin, and I'd suddenly grown breasts—before anyone else. I tried to hide them. I slouched until my already bad posture became humpbacked.

In elementary school in Tehran, when I'd still had smooth skin and a flat chest, I had sometimes talked to boys. They were the children of foreigners, or of Iranians who'd lived abroad, or a mix of both, like me. We spoke English at school, which set us apart from most Tehranis. By sixth grade we were tentatively chatting during free periods, asking each other about homework. By high school we would have started dating. But halfway through sixth grade, the Islamic revolution closed our school, cut short our budding courtships, and scattered us across the globe.

My family ended up in Portland, Oregon, where kids wore Izod shirts and Sperry Top-Siders and pink and green grosgrain watchbands. The revolution had left my family unable to afford much for my wardrobe, but my mother understood the importance of fitting in. She had grown up the daughter of a Beverly Hills psychoanalyst; her classmates had been children of movie directors. Money had not been a problem for her, nor had fitting in.

I, on the other hand, came from a place that, two months after I started seventh grade at a new school, decided to give my social life a boost by taking fifty-two Americans hostage. Across the country, trees got yellow ribbons and Iranian students got beaten up. I slunk down the halls wishing my name were Katharine, wishing I'd grown up in the States and knew what everyone else knew.

And then one day my mother produced for me something no other girl had: A real preppy. Stephen was the son of our neighbors. I had never met him because he was a student at Kent, a Connecticut boarding school that was actually listed in *The Official Preppy Handbook*. Stephen's little brother was friends with my little brother, and his mother was friends with my mother. He was coming home for a holiday, and the mothers had devised a plan that my mom perhaps thought would make up for the opportunities I'd missed because of the revolution—the parties I hadn't been invited to in my new school, the boys who had overlooked me in favor of other girls.

Stephen, the prep school boy, would take me on a date. Skiing.

I had been skiing once, in the mountains outside Tehran. It was a school trip, and instructors were not provided, but I spent a couple of days happily sailing down bunny hills and, clueless about how to stop, throwing my body to the ground like a giant brake. I came home bruised but exhilarated and announced I loved skiing.

Now I'd be skiing with Stephen of the Kent School. He'd be an expert skier, I imagined; he'd take my arm and teach me to glide in elegant serpentine waves and stop in a glamorous spray of diamonds. In the lodge afterward, flushed with sun and wind, we'd sit by the fire drinking hot toddies, whatever they were.

Stephen was fifteen, so a bus was found to take us the hour and a half to Mount Hood. When Stephen and his mom arrived in the chilly predawn darkness to drive me to the bus, I had a flash of dread: What was I doing? Who were these people? I hardly even knew his mother, a thin-lipped woman with a smoker's rasp.

"Shut up," I hissed to myself. This was not a time to be shy. This was a time to be charming, to smile, to engage in bright repartee.

His mother introduced us.

"Hi," we said.

I slid into the back seat of their car, my mind racing for what to say next.

Stephen was kind of cute, with floppy blond bangs, a straight nose, and a faint Slavic tilt to his eyes. On the bus, we took seats near the front, and, hoping to get the conversation flowing, I summoned a question.

"How long are you in town?"

"A week."

The bus drove on. The sky lightened, and after a while snow started to appear along the edges of the road. I blurted out, "Hey look, snow!"

Stephen nodded. My face burned. Of course there would be snow—we were going skiing. And a guy from Connecticut was not going to be impressed with a little snow.

Trying to cover up my blunder, I started babbling. "It hasn't snowed in Portland at all this year," I said. Then I remembered two things we had in common—brothers and dogs—and decided to introduce them into the conversation.

"Last year we had a huge ice storm and your brother came sledding with us," I said. "He brought your dogs, and our dog came, and they were all running with the sled."

Stephen said nothing.

Then, after a minute, he said, "Those aren't my dogs. They're my stepfather's."

Maybe, I thought, he would warm up on the slopes.

When we got to the ski lodge, we rented equipment and Stephen looked at a trail map. "Let's take this," he said, and I followed him to a chairlift. We floated over white slopes and pine groves. The air was clean and silent. *Okay,* I thought, *now is the time to talk.*

"So, are you a good skier?"

He shrugged. Which could have meant yes. Or no. Either way, it was his turn. I glanced at him expectantly. He had on big yellow goggles that hid his eyes.

I was nervous about getting off the lift, but when it deposited us at the top I proudly skied off without falling. Then, standing at the top of the mountain, Stephen uttered the longest sentence he'd said all day: "See you at the bottom."

Wait a minute! What about me? I still couldn't see Stephen's eyes, but as he glided away, something in the slope of his Slavic cheekbones, in the curt nod of his head, told me something was wrong. I'd never dated before, but this, I knew, was not how a boy was supposed to treat his date. This was not the way my father had treated my mother on their first date, which I knew all about—the tomato and salami sandwiches on the beach, the sharing of secrets, the sunset at the end of a perfect day. Abandonment on a mountaintop was not remotely close.

Stephen receded toward a clump of trees, crested a small hill, and disappeared.

I stood alone. Or not entirely alone; near me was a signpost. Further down, the runs had been marked with green and blue circles and squares; this sign had two black diamonds. And a name: Elevator Shaft.

I looked down. The run actually didn't look too bad. If I went slowly I could probably make it. I crouched down and leaned one side of my body toward the mountain. Aiming unsteadily for the trees and the small mound where I'd last seen Stephen, I felt heartened. This was a double-black-diamond run, but I was managing it, graceless but unscathed.

And then I beheld the Shaft.

It was almost vertical, a half-tube. Snow had been scraped away in spots to reveal smudges of black dirt and rocks. Hemmed between groves of trees, it plunged far down before turning right. God knew what lay beyond that. I looked up at the ski lift. It was too far to get back to. I looked at the trees, but they were on higher ground, and following them would strand me. The only way down was down.

I tipped my skis forward.

I immediately started sliding. Panicked, I did the only thing I knew to do on skis: threw myself on the ground. By digging various body parts into the snow, I managed to grind to a stop.

And there I stayed. All that mattered was not moving. If I did, I might not be able to stop again, but would gather speed and start rolling until I became one of those giant snowballs that, in cartoons, end by flying off a cliff or crashing into a house.

I didn't feel cold; the shaft blocked the wind, and my adrenaline was pumping. I wasn't scared as much as baffled, as if I was in a movie whose plot had veered off into senselessness. How would I get out of this? Would Stephen notice I wasn't behind him? Would he come back for me?

He didn't.

Instead, after a few minutes, some other skiers appeared. A man stopped and asked if I was all right. "Oh yeah, I'm fine," I said, affecting a blasé, isn't-this-silly air, though I was relieved. Cool and calm was how I wanted to come across. But I also didn't want him to think I was content to keep lying there, so I added, "I just can't get down the mountain."

Promising help, he disappeared down the shaft.

Half an hour later two young men in red coats appeared. They were older and cuter than Stephen, burly and tan, with the friendly manner of Labrador retrievers. My spirits lifted. Each of them would gallantly offer an arm, I imagined, and guide me safely through the shaft. By the bottom we'd be joking around, and I'd have learned some skiing tips, no thanks to Stephen.

Then I saw the stretcher. It lay on the ground, and they were telling me to get in it.

I'm not injured, I wanted to say. *I don't need to be carried. I can get down perfectly fine standing up, if you'll just show me how.* But I had caused enough trouble, so I said nothing.

Making sure no one was watching, I lay down in the stretcher. They swathed me in blankets. They cinched straps around the blankets. They picked me up and started down the mountain.

The shaft opened up onto a mountainside full of skiers, none of whom seemed to have anything better to do than swerve over to get a peek at the injured person. They approached cautiously, as if they might see death, or features contorted in agony. Instead, they saw a face red with shame and misery.

I prayed we would not pass Stephen. I didn't want him to see me like this, immobilized, dependent on others to save me from the spot he'd put me in. If leaving me on the mountain had been a test of my toughness, I'd failed. But I didn't want him to know that; I didn't want him to think he'd won whatever game it was that he was playing.

I don't remember what I did for the rest of the day, whether I practiced on bunny slopes or skulked around the lodge, mortified that someone might recognize me as the Stretcher Girl. At the end of the day I boarded the bus and found a window seat. Minutes later, Stephen got on. My face burned, but I pretended not to notice him, and watched from the corner of my eye to see where he'd sit. He slid into the seat beside me.

"Hi," he said, as if he'd just left me a minute ago.

In my head, I was bitingly sarcastic. *Thanks a lot. It was really fun. I had a great time crawling across the ice and having strangers carry me down.* But to say those things would be to admit I was upset, so I all I could muster was saying "hi" back, and then I looked at the road. I returned home too embarrassed to say what had happened. I told my mother the day had been fine, and I never saw Stephen again.

The following year I signed up for skiing lessons. I entered high school and started talking to boys. Some became my friends. One, a punk-rocker in a leather jacket, kissed me outside the drama room and asked me to be his girlfriend. Although my mother's heart sank every time I rode off, helmetless, on the back of his Vespa, she didn't try to set me up with anyone else.

Recently I asked if she remembered the ski date. At first she didn't, although she did remember Stephen's mother telling her he'd been sent away to school because he had emotional problems—a detail I'd never heard.

"I thought you liked skiing a lot," she said. "I don't remember anything about a stretcher."

She began to tell me about her own parents setting her up on disastrous dates, then stopped, realizing she had done the same to me.

"Well, sweetie," she finally said, "I love your instincts of self-preservation. It gives me a warm feeling that you can take care of yourself."

It must have been that feeling, all those years ago, that allowed her to send me off to a mountain in the dark with an emotionally disturbed teenager. Since I had gotten home that night and said nothing, she had never had the chance to say something comforting, to find some grace note in my day of clinging to an ice-swept rock face and shaming myself before a mountainful of strangers. She said it now instead, over a long-distance phone line.

"I'm proud of you," she said, "for going down on your butt."

Nice Girl's Guide to
Life and Death

Karen Alexander

They seemed interchangeable, the boys my mother set me up with. Short and stocky, tall and wiry, nervous, morose—they were probably nothing alike, but to me they were the same, smelling of Old Spice and adolescent desire and despair. Their faces, pink and acne-prone, were often bleeding from a recent shave. Their bodies seemed tightly packed into their skin, as if they might burst at any minute with something long pent-up. These were the boys who couldn't get dates on their own. Though awkward and embarrassed, they weren't completely without hope, and why should they have been? They were only fifteen or sixteen, with mothers who loved them, or at least worried about them; and it was their mothers who contacted my mother to set us up.

"Why me?" I asked my mother. "Because you're so nice," she said. She would then grow a little apologetic, but no less insistent. "Well perhaps he's a little shy," she'd say. But an angel in disguise. A diamond in the rough. A future champion of the world. And putty in your hands. If you liked putty.

Today, the idea of arranging dates for fourteen and fifteen year olds seems a little strange or prurient—at best, quite unnecessary. But this was in the late fifties and early sixties, an era still sprinkled faintly with the rusty glitter of the Gilded Age, when a girl needed to be married before her bloom was off. It was in this tradition that, as a pre-teen, I studied books entitled *How to Be Popular* (answer: smile all the time, at everyone) and went dutifully to cotillion class, where we learned how to cross our legs at the ankles and how to keep a dance card. I also completed the full course at Mr. Lynn's Charm School, where we learned "the model's walk," a difficult, languorous stride in which we rolled our feet "from the outside-in" while leaning backwards as if lying down: this would prepare us, if not for the fashion runway, at least for the greatest runway of them all—the walk down the aisle. The subtly lipsticked Mr. Lynn taught us this walk himself.

So that's the way it was. Every few months, the doorbell would ring. The good son would present himself with a corsage for me, sometimes flowers for my mother. Sometimes he would wear a suit, most of the time a cardigan sweater. We'd go to an Italian movie, or to Harry Belafonte at the Greek Theatre, or to a multi-course meal at Scandia. My assignment: to build the confidence of these young men, in much the way it was my mother's unspoken but essential mission to transform my father—a shy, uncommunicative psychoanalyst—into a warmer human being.

The summer I came home from my first year at Berkeley, I had no boyfriend, and my mother fixed me up again. "I really think you'll like him," she said, less apologetic than usual. For once, he was not the son of a Freudian, Jungian, or Kleinian. His father was a TV actor. And although in my small world actors did not quite have the status of psychiatrists, there was still some glamour attached to the idea of meeting Robbie N. Robbie's mother knew mine from the tennis club and wanted to invite me to dinner to meet her middle son, the one home from Stanford.

"I bet he'll be nice," my mother continued. "Louise is such a lovely woman." Clearly my mother thought I should be happy to meet the scion of minor Hollywood royalty. "Do it as a favor to me," she added. "We really don't ask much of you."

So I went. I was curious to meet the actor, the comically obsequious sidekick I'd seen in many a boring Western and cop show. And curious to meet Robbie, too, of course. The next Sunday evening, I drove to a sprawling, multi-winged house in the Palisades, where I was greeted by Robbie's father, smaller and older than he appeared on screen, but sweet, if a little depressed. Robbie's mother was incredibly pretty, with hair in a long graying pageboy. She twirled around in that musical, big-skirted, mid-century way, offering drinks and hors d'oeuvres, as if she would burst into song at any minute.

Robbie emerged from the shadows of a hallway, and we were directed to take a walk in the garden. I had only caught a glimpse of him in his house, but what I'd caught was not encouraging. He was tall, like his mother, with the tiny features of his cute little father planted somewhat unfortunately on his long, large face. His teeth were too big for his mouth, his eyes too small for his head. Feature for feature, he looked like his attractive parents, but something had gone awry in the distribution. He was handsome gone wrong, which was scarier than ugly.

We walked through the garden, taking surreptitious glances at each other as the sun went down. I kept my eyes mostly on the flowers and trees and asked him to identify them, which he did, expertly. Fuchsia, Freesia, Mandevilla, Tibouchina. "What's that?" I asked, pointing to a green and purple flower. "That's lettuce," he said. We both laughed, and relaxed a little. When we were done, we went on to movie stars. Who were the people who had come to this fabulous house when he was growing up? Robbie named them, relieved to have another area of expertise, sounding nonchalant, hoping to impress. Richard Widmark. Kirk Douglas. Burt Lancaster.

"What's he like?" I asked.

Robbie's answer was to draw his strange pale face into a wide grimace that was supposed to imitate Burt's toothy grin. But it more resembled the grin of Lon Cheney, unmasked in *Phantom of the Opera*. I had a vision of ten-year-old Robbie, flashing this very grin at the dinner table, getting approving laughs. But now, it wasn't as cute.

"Henry Miller's been here. He lives nearby. My brother brings girls to him." This was somewhat intriguing. "I used to take the school bus up Beverly Glen with Liza Minelli, he said. "She wore too much eye make-up, for a kid."

We agreed on that, but that was as much as we knew about her. It seemed that Robbie was running out of things to dazzle me with. He was nineteen, and this was nearly his last chance to ride on the glamour of his parent's magnificent garden and star-studded childhood.

"Dore Shary," he finally offered, out of nowhere. "And Gore Vidal."

I perked up.

"Dore and Gore," he said. I laughed. He laughed. Maybe he wasn't so bad.

We were still laughing as we came in for dinner. Robbie took his place in the dimly lit dining room, surrounded by his two stunning brothers and his amiable parents. While Robbie watched in silence, and his brothers made occasional jokes, his parents and I made small talk about what I was doing that summer—teaching remedial reading in Watts. They asked about college and my father's work.

After dinner, Robbie's mother hugged me in the kitchen, warmly and firmly. She stood back and looked at me, but not long enough to be rude. "What a nice girl you are," she said. There were real tears in her eyes.

Later, Robbie's father walked me to my car. "I think you and Rob might really hit it off," he said. "He's a great kid. Sensitive. Probably the nicest of my sons. He just needs someone to see it." And there I was, already cast in the part.

I drove home thinking I could do this. After all, he was leaving soon for a year abroad. I wouldn't have to break his heart. I could just administer some cheerful therapy and then say goodbye at an airport, leaving him ever-so-slightly improved, his ego bolstered, his pride intact. Newly confident for the girls of Europe and better prepared for the life he deserved—a life like that of his parents.

"How was it?" my mother asked when I got home. When I said it wasn't so bad, that Robbie's parents had a beautiful home and great family, she got up from the couch, and she too hugged me.

So, I went on a second date with Robbie N. He appeared at the door, smelling that usual first date way—extra showered with the soap-toothpaste-aftershave-mouthwash-deodorant-hair-cream smell. His black hair, long for those days, was greased back into a tall helmet. I was sympathetic and repulsed. My parents came into the hallway to meet the actor's son. They made small talk while I took a closer look at Robbie in a house more brightly lit than his own. He was clammy. He was bony. There was something glittery in his eyes. My parents both smiled approvingly, and I pictured Robbie's parents back in the darkened rooms of their grand ranch, also smiling approvingly, knowing Robbie was in good hands.

Robbie took me into the hills of the Palisades to a party, and then up to the hills of Bel Air to another party, and then up Coldwater Canyon, once again to a party. At each of these parties we had a drink, and I was introduced to ten or twenty people, many of them offspring of people in the entertainment business—the Mitchum boys, the Dragon boys, the daughters of Errol or Dinah. By the end of the evening, at least 150 people, Robbie's entire quota of acquaintances, had seen that he had a date. A date who was, by now, somewhat unsteady on her feet.

As we left the third party, Robbie led me across the crunching gravel, and when we got back in the car, he leaned in for a kiss. I leaned away, pressing myself into the side window. What's the big deal, I thought to myself. I could just kiss him. But, for some reason, I just couldn't. We sat there for a very long moment, staring at each other, and then, without a word, he started the motor and we took off onto the dark canyon road at fifty, then seventy or eighty miles per hour. Careening around the cliffs as in a bad spy movie, we sped on in the dark. It seemed there were no other cars, just me and Robbie on the road to oblivion.

They say that at such times, your past life flashes before you, but in my case, it was the life I hadn't had yet that made its appearance—the children I would never hold, the vague unarticulated ambitions that would never be fulfilled, the great world unexplored, and yes, my future as a woman who might finally know true love—all wrenched from me by this now stringy-haired madman. *I want to live*, I thought, as fervently as Susan Hayward had in the movie that had once so terrified me.

"This is crazy!" I screamed. "You're going to kill us both!"

"Yes!" hissed Robbie, his eyes animated by rage, his eyebrows creeping up and up his long forehead. His hair helmet had disintegrated and was now hanging in little spikes over his eyes. I wasn't sure he could even see the road. And he wasn't heading down the hill toward traffic, but up to the wilds of Mulholland Drive, with miles and miles to go before we would reach our ultimate rest, probably at the bottom of a gully.

I whined and pleaded and shouted. I calculated the risks of grabbing the wheel, of jumping. Freudian atheist that I was, I bargained with God. Finally a car came toward us, honking and blinking its lights, pulling off the road at the last minute and falling into a ditch.

"Aren't you going to stop?" I yelled. "Maybe they're hurt."

Robbie said nothing, but actually pressed down the accelerator a little more.

"Okay," I said, as we reached the crest of the mountain, as we screeched over on two tires and I looked down at the sparkling expanse of the San Fernando Valley, afraid it was the last thing I would ever see. "Okay, okay. I'll do whatever you want!" I screamed.

Robbie immediately slowed the car down, and as he rolled it under a lone tree perched on a smooth precipice that faced the Valley, I jumped out and started running.

"Hey, you tricked me!" I think he said. Or it maybe it was just "Hey you. . . ." I was making good time down the road, not yet having figured out what I would do next. My high heels in my hand, my stiff party dress rustling in the night wind, my rapid, huffy stride on a lonely mountain road famous as a lovers' lane—all this clearly advertised my plight as damsel in distress. And my rescue came almost immediately. The first car that stopped to offer help was that of an elderly couple—he with bald head and bow tie, his wife wearing a little hat with a veil over her tight, white curls and, most auspiciously, a limp, dead fox around her neck—the kind of outfit my own grandmother wore. The little fox feet dangled like lucky charms as she asked, "Do you need a ride somewhere?"

Well, they could have been killers in clever disguise, but I took a chance. "No need to explain," said the man, who smelled comfortingly of cigar and tweed.

"Yes," said his wife. "We've all been there." She laughed—her voice the perpetually delighted, tremulous trill of Glinda the Good Witch. They drove me down Benedict Canyon and dropped me off at the Beverly Wilshire, where I got a cab home.

My father greeted me at the door, with a drink in his hand. My mother, also holding a drink, leaned gracefully on the couch with her ankles crossed.

"Have a good time?" she said sweetly.

"Not really." I said.

"Oh, too bad," said my father. "I really like that Robbie. He reminds me of myself at that age. I can tell he's kind of fragile, so I hope you'll be nice to him."

I didn't want to insult my father, who had just revealed himself so uncharacteristically, so I said nothing. Perhaps I groaned.

"Maybe he'll improve with age," my father said.

"Or not," said my mother. "Maybe he'll get worse."

Maybe, I thought, as I made my way, exhausted, up the stairs to my room. And maybe the next time they ask if they could fix me up, I'd say, as nicely as I could: No.

The Man of My Dreams
Will Have None of My Genes

Rachel Pine

"Tell me again how he's not my cousin?" I asked my mother, who was now explaining it to me for the sixth time.

It had been fifteen minutes since she'd first suggested I have dinner with this guy I'd always thought of as my cousin, albeit a couple of times removed by marriage.

"Rachel, he is *not* your cousin," my mother said into the receiver. "You have cousins in common, but the two of you *are not cousins*!" she added, her voice rising with exasperation at the end. I was entering the red zone.

It's easy to understand why I considered David to be my cousin. He and his parents, along with his rude sister, were at most family events hosted by my father's side. Not by my father, but by his *side*, as my mother was always quick to point out. As a rule my mother didn't care much for David's clan. But isn't spending time with people you don't like the definition of "relative"? Whether or not we shared blood or DNA or ancestors, David felt sort of cousinish, which is how I began to refer to him in my mind: Cousin Ish.

I was very suspicious. Why was my mother setting me up with a guy who came from a family she couldn't stand? Besides, if we were going to go all *Deliverance*, there were definitely better candidates. I've got lots of cousins.

"Mommy, I thought you didn't like them."

"Well, I don't, but Pearl—you know Pearl, his grandmother? She says he's a genius and that he's gotten very handsome. She thinks you and David will have a lot in common. You both like books."

Cousin Ish liked books. I liked books. What's not to like?

"Right. A handsome genius who likes books but needs his grandmother to fix him up," I said. Obviously, Cousin Ish couldn't get a date and I was a twenty-year-old spinster. The fact that my mother was worried, worried me.

It had been four months since I'd graduated from college and started my first job. While I hadn't yet taken the city's eligible men by storm, I had no reason to believe that I wasn't about to. I just needed to figure out how.

The only piece of dating advice I'd ever received from my mother was, "Don't settle." She'd drummed it into my head from the time I was a pre-teen. "Never settle. Don't ever settle on someone who isn't just right." Was this her vision of "just right"?

I hadn't seen Cousin Ish since he was twelve and I was ten, at a Thanksgiving Day dinner hosted by my father's sister. He was skinny, with freckles, wearing too-short cords, white socks, and sneakers, with wire-rimmed glasses perched on the end of his nose. I'd been dressed nearly identically, minus the eyeglasses. We were both kind of square and on the cusp of understanding that everything about our respective parents was utterly repulsive. That was the last Thanksgiving we'd spent together. Something happened—I never knew what it was, and after that we always had Thanksgiving with my mother's family.

I sat on the edge of my couch imagining what was taking place as my mother started the process. I pictured it in the style of a '70s sitcom, with each person in a different bubble to indicate that they are not in the same place. My mother on the phone/ Pearl on the phone (bubble with Ish, reading a book, completely unaware that he is at the center of all this activity)/they hang up/my mother disappears/Pearl dials/Cousin Ish pops up with an audible "ploof" and a phone in his hand. In the TV show in my head, he looked exactly as he did at twelve. I changed the channel.

The phone rang and I waited for exactly four trills before answering—sufficient time, I was sure, to lead the caller to understand that I was a woman with a wealth of both things to do and apartment space.

"Um, hello, is Rachel there?" said a man's voice.

"This is she," I answered crisply, not recognizing the voice.

"It's David."

His voice had changed, I thought, hopeful in spite of myself. I realized that this set-up stuff had reduced me from a reasonably confident young woman to someone who was grateful that a twenty-two-year-old had exited puberty.

"It's been a while."

"Um, my grandmother said that I should call you," he half-stammered. I was glad that I wasn't the only uncomfortable one.

"Right. My mother told me they'd been talking."

"What else does my grandmother do?"

I laughed and so did he.

"So, um, my grandmother says you work with books?"

"Yes, I'm an editorial assistant at a book publisher. I just started a few months ago. What are you doing?"

"I'm getting my masters in computer science."

I asked him where and he named a school in midtown that I didn't think was accredited. Besides, didn't computer geniuses go to MIT?

"So you're living in the city?"

"No, actually, I'm living home while I finish. I only have to come in two days a week, so it made more sense than renting an apartment. It's only about seventy-five minutes on the bus from Rockland County."

"I live in Manhattan. On 28th Street and 9th Avenue," I said, feeling smug.

"Yeah, my father told me that Marion was letting you live in her apartment for the winter while she was in Florida."

Damn! Marion was my father's aunt. Of course he would know.

"Well, in the spring I'm moving to Cobble Hill with one of my friends from college."

"That's nice," he said, sounding genuine. "I have one more semester after this one and then I'm going to get a job, but I don't want to stay in New York."

Suddenly this had possibilities. If we liked each other and he moved away, there would be no end to the drama, the longing, and the phone bills. Flights would be courtesy of my mother, I was sure. And if he liked me but I didn't like him, I could say that I didn't want to be in a long-distance relationship, which was something I'd always wanted to say to someone but never had. And if we didn't like each other, things would be tied up nicely.

"Yeah, well, it's not for everyone," I said.

"Most of the big software firms are out in Jersey, anyway, so New York doesn't make sense for me."

My scenarios evaporated.

After that, we dealt with the logistics. We decided to have dinner a week from Tuesday in a Chinese restaurant midway between his school and my office.

I didn't tell anyone about this upcoming rendezvous. Blind dates were bad enough. Blind dates arranged by your mother were worse. And blind dates arranged by your mother with someone who was sort of your relative were decidedly outside the realm of the shareable.

When I arrived at the restaurant Cousin Ish was standing right inside the door. "Rachel?"

"David! It's nice to see you." I wasn't lying. Cousin Ish had left his nerdy self behind, maybe on a bus somewhere on the way down from Rockland County. He had filled out and while he wasn't exactly buff, he wasn't spindly, either. The glasses were gone and he had nice blue eyes with very long lashes. Just a smattering of freckles remained, giving him a bit of an out-doorsy, healthy look. He was wearing a sweater over a button-down shirt and jeans that met the tops of his loafers, which he wore on his bare feet. This was the late 1980s, so his lack of socks earned him major style points. I was dressed like what I was: A girl from Queens working at her first job in Manhattan. Think *Working Girl* minus the ferry. Blazer with big shoulder pads. Even bigger hair. "Nude" pantyhose.

"You look really different," he said.

"Well, it's been ten years. I hope I do." I had breasts now.

He took my hand and sort of shook it. I could tell he didn't know what to do, but to be fair, neither did I.

We walked to our table and sat down. A waiter brought over fried noodles and duck sauce, and Ish dove in with gusto.

"I love these! And they're free!" He munched happily and had soon finished the bowl. The waiter replaced it with another bowlful and pointed to the menus. "Oh yeah. How about we share an appetizer and an entrée? They just give you so much food at these places."

"Sure, I guess." He was obviously going to substitute the free fried noodles for an actual dish.

"Do you know what you want?" he asked through a mouthful of noodles.

"Probably something with chicken—chicken and asparagus is my favorite."

"Oh," he sounded disappointed. "I was hoping you'd say broccoli."

Well, we both still liked books. "It's okay, I eat broccoli. Just order what you want and I'm sure it will be fine." It wasn't as if I would be getting a whole plate of it, anyway.

The waiter took our order. "And for you, miss?" he said, when David had finished.

"We're sharing," David said.

"Nothing else for you?" the waiter asked. I wanted to ask for something—steamed wontons, specifically, but opted for a side of martyrdom instead.

Our spring rolls arrived and Ish tucked in, dipping his roll into an elaborate mixture he'd made of duck sauce, soy sauce, and hot mustard. I took a spring roll and cut it in half, ever so daintily. There were now just two left on the plate, and at that moment I determined to eat them both, just for spite.

"Do you remember all those Thanksgivings in your Aunt Selma's apartment?" he asked.

"Of course." Selma was my father's older sister. She thought herself quite the glamour-puss—always in sky-high Candie's sandals and never without a cigarette. "You know that Selma is older than my father, right?" I said, reaching for a second spring roll.

"I thought so, but I wasn't sure," David said. "My mother said she liked to lie about her age."

"I think even she's lost track," I said. "One year my mother told her, 'Selma, keep it up and next year you'll be a fetus.'"

"Your mother says what's on her mind," he said as I reached for the last spring roll. "That's mine," he said briskly, grabbing it from just under my fingers.

"My mother doesn't tolerate bullshit," I said, wondering why her daughter was doing just that. "And definitely not from my father's family."

When the entrée came, David loaded his plate up with chicken and broccoli from the serving dish. He topped it off with an entire bowlful of rice.

I began to move what was left onto my plate and David snapped at me again.

"Hey, don't eat everything," he said, motioning at the serving dish.

I put one broccoli spear back with an elaborate flourish of chopsticks intended to demonstrate my dismay.

"Do you ever talk to our delightful cousins?" he asked, ignoring my theatrics. I shuddered at the "our" in the sentence.

"Not if I can avoid it. We don't have much to do with them. You?"

"Well, my parents' place in Florida is near Selma's so I see them once or twice each winter."

"Lucky you," I said. He grimaced.

After our plates were cleared the waiter stopped by with fortune cookies and the check.

"Are you going to eat that?" He pointed at my fortune cookie. I grabbed it and broke it open, and my fortune fell on the floor. It was just as well, I thought, happily crunching away. I couldn't bear to do the "in bed" thing with him.

I asked him if he'd like to split the check. He looked offended. "Of course not. I never take a girl out and expect her to pay."

I bit my tongue to stop myself from asking if he expected her to eat.

"Besides," he said. "My father gave me money for tonight."

"Thank him for me," I said, smiling sweetly before adding, "I really have to run now." I couldn't put my coat on fast enough.

"What's the hurry?" he said, following me out the door and onto the street. "Do you want to take a walk in Central Park or something?"

"No thanks. I'm just going to go home."

"Can I walk with you?" he fell into step beside me. We walked a few blocks, and then he turned to me, and said, "I'd really like to see you again. Can I call you?"

"I don't know if that's a good idea," I said. "I'm kind of seeing someone." I'd always wanted to say that to someone and he looked confused, as if he knew I was lying, but didn't know why.

"It was nice to see you again," I said, before heading off home, alone. "And thanks for dinner."

I was still in my coat when I dialed my mother. I told her most of the story, and said, "I think he made a *profit*. I'm sure his father gave him more than ten bucks for dinner."

"You know, I never liked them," she said.

"I know that. We've established that. What I don't understand is why you wanted me to go out with him?"

"I wanted to see if Pearl was telling the truth—is he as handsome and smart as she said?"

"Yes. He's like Einstein, but hot. A hot Einstein." I knew this would upset her.

My mother gasped. "You're kidding!"

"No, really, Mommy. David's a totally hot, cheap, Einstein. He can win the Nobel Prize in physics *and* economics," I said taunting her, starting to giggle. After I'd stopped laughing I said, "You know, I'm not going to settle, not even for a hot Einstein if he's not generous."

I made her swear to never fix me up again. Even at times when I could see that she was physically having difficulty keeping her mouth shut, she kept her promise.

As for my Cousin Ish? We don't really hear from that side of the family.

You'll Have a Wonderful Life with Him

Rochelle Jewel Shapiro

When I was only sixteen, my mother tried to hand me over to Leonard Silbergould whose mother she'd met in a Canasta game at the home of our across-the-street neighbor, Nessie Kleinkoph.

"Your grandmother was married at twenty," my mother said. "I was married at twenty, and so was my sister. And you aren't going to be single a day longer than that," she added, her thinly plucked eyebrows bouncing up and down on her forehead in time with the clacking of her knitting needles. She had three daughters, all widely spaced. She thought the longer she waited between each one increased the chances for her having the son that my father claimed he needed in order to be happy.

By 1963, my two older sisters were already married (one at twenty, the other at eighteen.) My mother was forty-eight by then, worked six long days a week in my father's grocery, and had an eight-year-old to take care of (the boy my father had always hoped for.) My father was no happier than he'd been before "The Messiah," as he called him, was born. After the birth, my mother had had to have four scrapings and a double hernia operation. To lighten her load, she wanted to marry me off to someone well-to-do so I'd never show up at her doorstep, wanting for anything.

At nineteen, Leonard Silbergould was a junior in college, an honor student, premed. (He'd skipped a year of elementary school, one of junior high, and had taken accelerated courses in high school.) "After medical school, he's going into brain surgery," my mother announced.

I rolled my eyes. "Mom, I don't need you to run my life."

"Oh, really?" she said, frowning.

I didn't answer. I knew I was trouble for my mother. My first boyfriend, Vick, had been a Juvenile Delinquent who'd stolen all my father's silver dollars over the course of the six months he'd helped me babysit my brother. And I smoked cigarettes and hung around with a girl whose big sister's boyfriend was in jail. I did need guidance, but the only guidance my mother gave me was "date Leonard Silbergould." She'd phone me from my father's grocery store to remind me to pick my brother up at the bus stop, defrost the box of flounder fillets, and "give Leonard Silbergould a chance, why don't you?"

At night she'd come into my room and whisper in my ear, "You'll have a wonderful life with Leonard Silbergould." After awhile, I couldn't tell whether he was her dream or mine.

I finally said "yes" after she'd threatened to revoke a weekend program at Pratt Institute for high school students gifted in art. Plus she wore me down with her nagging that Nessie Kleikoph's daughter, Harriet, would snap him up and I'd miss my chance.

My mother happily gave Mrs. Silbergould our number. That night, Leonard phoned to ask me if I'd like to go to the movies with him on Saturday night.

"I hope you don't mind walking," he said. "I'm going to give my parents their car for the evening." He chuckled, so I guessed he'd made a joke.

"Okay," I said, and he took down my address and told me he'd pick me up at seven.

My mother brought me to the beauty parlor to straighten my frizzy hair. She bought me Pappagallo shoes at Jildor and a pink blouse. She insisted I wear a skirt instead of jeans, but I refused. We settled on a pair of culottes that had front and back panels. It looked pretty much like a skirt unless you took big steps.

Saturday night Leonard Silbergould showed up wearing a light blue button-down shirt and chinos. He was tall and lanky, with dark hair and mica eyes. His intense gaze and his smile—a quick jerk of his cheek muscles—made me shiver with aversion.

"I'm Leonard Silbergould," he said, as if I needed to be reminded. "And you must be Rochelle, the one I've heard so much about." I nodded. "How very nice to meet you," he said, holding out a bunch of daisies, the stems wrapped in wax paper and secured with a rubber band.

I wanted to run into my bedroom, lock the door, and hide, but my mother, reeking of Evening in Paris toilet water and all dressed up in her silk jungle-print sheath, stepped forward and took the flowers from him.

"How very sweet of you," she gushed. "Perhaps you'd like to come for dinner on Sunday night. I'm making my pot roast."

"Night, Mom," I said firmly and hustled Leonard out the door.

My mother had told me, "You're not used to talking to decent fellahs, so take a tip from me. Just ask him about himself and he'll be happy."

I didn't have to. As soon as we were out of my gate, Leonard bragged about how he'd scored the highest you could on his

SATs, and how many colleges had offered him full scholarships, and how every Ivy had accepted him, but he'd decided on NYU so he could have lunch with his father who worked nearby.

In the days before the Cineplex, our town—Rockaway Beach, Queens, in New York City—had two movie theaters. I wanted to see *Bye Bye Birdie*, but he insisted on *Diary of a Madman*.

Once inside, when he didn't offer to buy popcorn or soda, I thought, *Well, he's got a year more of college and then the expense of all those years of medical school.* Vick had always bought me popcorn and soda and anything else I wanted, but after all, I reminded myself, it had been with stolen money.

"Let's sit in the balcony," Leonard said. "That way, the matron won't be shining her flashlight on us if we talk."

Talk? Maybe he'd chosen a lousy film because he wanted to get to know me, I thought as he led me up the steps of the balcony seats into the last row.

When the lights dimmed, he said, "I'm glad you wore a skirt."

He's just like my mother, I thought, but suddenly, he pressed his hand into my crotch, digging into the seam of my culottes. I was so shocked I froze. A guy was supposed to give you great kisses and start touching you at the top, then work his way down slowly, giving you lots of time to push his hand away or say no. Not only was Leonard Silbergould a make-out cretin, everything about him was, what we called back then, "vomitatious."

"This isn't a real skirt," he complained, his hand groping around, looking for some kind of opening.

That snapped me out of my paralysis. "Hey!" I finally said, yanking his hand away. "Don't you dare!"

Even in the dark I could see his face redden with rage. "The only reason I agreed to go out with you," he said, his voice rising, "was that I heard you were fast."

Heads were turning to look at me. Over the railing of the balcony, I saw people standing up, trying to see. Crossing my legs tightly, I shrunk into my seat. I thought Leonard's outburst was over, but he was only warming up.

"The whole town knows that you went out with a hood and that you smoke and hang out with that Patsy McElroy. Hey, is her sister's boyfriend still in jail by the way?"

On the screen, Vincent Price was being threatened by an evil spirit, but I was at the movies with one. Nobody was telling Leonard to be quiet. They were too interested in what he had to say. Even the matron was standing in the aisle, just listening.

I sprang up. "The only reason why I went out with you," I said, "was that my mother made me." I tried to get out of the row as quickly and discreetly as possible, but the matron appeared, shinning her flashlight in my face for the audience to see. Leonard just sat there watching the movie.

I walked home by myself, imagining with each step that everyone who passed me, either by foot or in a car, was staring at me, pointing, and whispering, "There goes the town tramp." I was humiliated, but it never occurred to me to give up what had earned me a bad reputation. Instead, I swore to myself that in the future, I'd only date guys out of the neighborhood.

My mother, waiting for me at the door, demanded to know what happened. I couldn't tell her what Leonard had done because then she'd only blame me. Besides, anything having to do with sex, you just didn't tell my mother who still called a vagina a "hoo hoo."

"I'm just not attracted to him," I told her.

She threw up her hands. "Oh, you'll be so sorry someday that you gave up Leonard Silbergould," she said, and began to sob as if my whole life and hers were over.

As my mother predicted, Leonard Silbergould began dating Harriet Kleinkoph. Even though it killed my mother to see them together, she couldn't help watching out a slit in the blinds on a Saturday night for Leonard to walk up the Kleinkoph's slate path and ring their bell, and then wait for him and Harriet to go out together.

"No wonder Harriet hooked Leonard," my mother reported. "She at least knows to wear a regular skirt on a date."

A year later the two were married. Harriet was a very smart girl, but instead of going to college as she'd planned, she became a secretary to help pay Leonard's medical school bills.

The next year, I ran into her as she was on her way to her mother's house. I didn't recognize her at first. She seemed shorter. As I got closer, I realized it was because her shoulders were hunched. We had never been friendly, but I gave her a big cheery hello. I didn't want her to think I harbored bad feelings because I hadn't snagged Leornard. To my surprise, she grabbed my arm.

"Do I look as if I've been crying?" she asked desperately.

Her green eyes were red-rimmed and her lids were puffy. "Yes," I said. "What's wrong?"

"Please don't tell anyone," she said. "Especially not your mother. She'll tell mine and I just don't want my mother to know. She'll make everything worse."

"I'm great at keeping secrets from my mother," I assured her.

"Leonard says I'm dumb," she said, sniffing back tears. "He says we have nothing in common and he can't bear to listen to me anymore."

I was eighteen by then. No married woman had ever confided in me before. Once my sisters were married, they only confided in each other. I was flattered. "Maybe after Leonard finishes medical school, you can go to college," I said. "After all, when he's a doctor, you'll want for nothing."

Harriet brightened up. She pinched color into her cheeks and thanked me. "I was just being silly. You know it's that time of the month."

I was glad to have helped her, but she never got to act on my advice. By the next year, Leonard left her for another woman whose father was a big lawyer, chummy with all the judges. The divorce was over in a blink. I never said a word to anyone, but somehow it got all over town that Leonard thought Harriet was dumb.

"Poor Leonard," my mother said, "he would have been so much happier with you. I looked up his number," she said and handed me the phone. "Look, he's not remarried yet. Be sure to tell him that when you graduate college you're planning to go for a master's degree in art history. It will help if he knows you're smart."

I didn't make the call, and the following year Leonard's new wife filed an order of protection against him. I never told my mother about Leonard's behavior. I let her keep the illusion that we'd both have been happy with him. I continued to keep every secret from her that I could, especially the ones about the bad boys I dated who lived in other towns.

But the god who watches over lost girls must have had his eye on me. There had been a smart, funny, upstanding guy who I'd met at the beach that year. *He's not my type*, I told myself, but he kept asking me out. One day I said yes and was surprised at how buzzed I got when he kissed me at the end of the evening. With my old boyfriends, I'd ridden on the backs of speeding motorcycles, and scaled tall, spear-topped metal fences to defy "No Trespassing" signs. With this guy, I discovered the thrill of going bike riding in Central Park and climbing to the top of the Statue of Liberty.

We got married a few days before my twenty-first birthday. It was a date I had gotten without any help from my mother.

"He'll never make the money that Leonard Silbergould will," my mother scoffed.

But, forty years later, I'm still delighted to be with my husband and not Leonard Silbergould.

Nice, Jewish Boys

Samantha Levy

Blind dating is like getting a perm. When I was twelve, I begged my mother to let me curl my hair, and after she finally agreed, I flipped through every fashion magazine in the house and ripped out countless headshots. When the big day came, I marched into the salon, showed my hairdresser a shampoo ad with spiral, Shirley Temple–esque curls, and furiously grinned. I looked at myself in the mirror one final time, thanked God my days of straight, boring, mousy locks were over, and let my hairstylist do her thing. The moment before the metamorphosis started was exhilarating. A rush of adrenaline. The hope that this event just might change my life.

Blind dates were no different. Each time I looked in the mirror before one, I still got that blast of feelings—excitement and nerves all jumbled together. And I'd think, much like I did that day at the salon, that this blind date would bring the end of singledom, that this guy would be *the one*.

I think it boils down to the fact that I'm an idealist. Or, alternatively, extremely pathetic. Either way, in the spring of 2003, I was a senior in college, living with my parents in southern New Jersey, working part-time at the Olive Garden, and full-time snorting anything I could crush. I had just broken up with a 6'5" football player I met in a poetry class (as paradoxical as that sounds, he was actually a gifted poet) and was moping around the house penning sonnets about our tragic, short-lived love affair.

Enter, stage left: my mother, Francine. Now, to my detriment, I'm the spitting image of my father, a true Levy: round face, linebacker shoulders, and a flat chest. My mother, however, is beautiful. She is petite and busty, with short, spiky blonde hair and full, blush lips. She's also loud, opinionated, neurotic—your run-of-the-mill Jewish mom. She wasn't a fan of the football player; he wasn't Jewish nor did he chew with his mouth closed. So her quest—which had been put on hiatus during those few months I wore all black and extra-high high heels—resumed: She would find me a nice, Jewish boy.

This is what I knew: Joel was Jewish, a few years older than me, and a graduate student at the University of Pennsylvania studying something scientific and boring, albeit lucrative, in nature. He liked the Jersey Shore, was a Philadelphia Eagles fan, and played guitar in a band. His mother ran into mine at a mutual friend's wedding shower, and over orange-Stoli cosmopolitans and a bit of *yenta*-like behavior, a date was struck.

When my mother told me all this, I wasn't aggravated or upset at her for meddling; I was tickled! The thought of dating a musician perked my interest, and I'm an Eagles fan and degenerate gambler, too. And this was, after all, an excuse to wear heels and globs of mascara, a short skirt, and my green newsboy hat from Ann Taylor. Not to mention, the prize of all prizes: this may lead to a boyfriend. Because, let's face it, ever since watching *The Princess Bride* as a child, I've always been secretly searching for my own fairy tale, someone to rescue me from rodents of unusual size.

I let my mother take over: She put me on a week-long diet of water and broccoli and made an appointment to get my roots done. On the night of the date, she insisted I change outfits ten times and begged me to, "Just try on the girdle. You'll see." One temper tantrum, another outfit, and three layers of blush later, the doorbell rang.

"Wait here," my mother said. "Make an entrance. Sell it."

I heard the door creek open and the gushing begin: "You are so handsome," and "Look how tall you are," and "What a nice shirt that is." I closed my eyes and prayed she wouldn't say something like, "So, how big is your shmeckle?" I glanced in the mirror and messed with my hair, thoughts of princes galloping on white horses fleeted by, and I went downstairs.

I was pleasantly surprised by Joel's appearance (how cute would you expect a science geek to be?). He was tall and fit, incredibly tan with blue eyes and chiseled cheekbones, dressed spiffy yet casual in a button down and khakis, and his hair was just shaggy enough to say, "Yeah, I'm in a band, whatever." I quickly got panicky and tripped down the last three steps.

My mother laughed nervously and said, almost apologetically, "She's a bit of a klutz." Then she shoved my jacket at me, whispered in my ear not to eat like a pig, and we were off.

Joel took me to an Italian place in Philly where we ordered pizza and a bottle of wine. Not only was he handsome and smart, but he was also incredibly engaging. We talked and talked and it seemed as though we were the same person: We both loved blackjack and Broadway musicals and margaritas on the rocks, and neither of us knew how to swim.

"It's like, I've always known you. Or something," I said, and immediately I felt my cheeks flush at that ridiculous statement.

But then Joel said, "Yeah. I know what you mean." He served me a slice of pizza and refilled my glass of wine and those infamous clichés—lumps in throats and butterflies in bellies—engulfed me. The whole thing was completely dreamy.

The schism didn't occur until we hit politics: Joel was a bonafide Republican. After he admitted this, I let the wine do the talking.

"Are you serious?" I asked. "You're in your twenties. You're supposed to be a Democrat."

Joel wasn't having any of that. He became passionate, spouting his philosophies and beliefs like a newscaster, point by point, calm and articulate. He talked with his hands, made a pie graph in the air when he discussed the pros of the war in Iraq, explained the benefits of a society without welfare.

And although I'm a Democrat, I subscribe to *People* magazine, not *Newsweek* or *Time*. So I fought back the only way I knew how: the silent treatment. I fidgeted, played with my napkin, folded then unfolded it, let the silence resonate. It was awkward and uncomfortable, this minute of quiet, the first conversation gap of the evening. Unexpectedly, he jumped up. I thought he was going to bolt for the door, but instead he took hold of my hands, knelt in place, and started to sing, loudly, "If I Could Turn Back Time."

At first, I was frozen, dumbstruck, mortified—wanted to grab the bottle of wine and chug. Is there an appropriate way to react, a protocol of some sort, when your date belts out Cher in the middle of a restaurant? Much less in a baritone voice while cupping your cheeks and bopping about like a flighty schoolgirl? He was loud and rehearsed like an overzealous, overdramatic karaoke singer, even doing the Cher toss as if he had long, flat-ironed hippie hair.

But then I realized all I wanted to do was run my fingers through that gorgeous, thick mane, so I smiled feverishly at this. I imagined him doing the same thing at our wedding—serenading me about how it was love at first sight! A song he wrote just for me—on one knee in a white tux!

After dinner, Joel and I went to a bar in Old City where we did shots and smoked cigarettes and sat inches apart. It was here that he made the confession of the night: "My mom used to powder my bottom until I was in the eighth grade."

I don't recall exactly how this little tidbit fit into the conversation, nor do I know if my drink fully came out of my nose or merely burned it. I do recollect, however, the knot in my stomach thinking about some middle-aged woman telling her adolescent son to lie on a fluffy towel in the bathroom and lift his legs over his head. I wondered if this task was like using insect repellent. Did his mother have to hold the powder at least twelve inches from his butt? And did she rub it in or simply sprinkle it around the general area?

"What did she powder it with?" I asked.

"Baby powder," he said wryly, as if I had asked the time.

"The white kind?"

He nodded. I drained my drink. Then ordered another.

We drank quite a bit by the end of the night, as blind dates usually recommend. Joel was in no position to drive me home, and despite the Cher and baby powder red flags, I was overcome with something—intrigue? Lust? Tequila?

"I could stay the night," I offered.

He shrugged. "Okay."

I read his trepidation as thoughtful embarrassment, like he forgot to buy condoms or left dirty dishes on his nightstand.

I don't remember the cab ride to his place or where exactly in Philadelphia he lived, but I do remember the smooching— clumsy yet tender, the kind of kissing that, I'm sure, made everyone in the bar want to applaud. This behavior continued in the car, at the front door, down the hallway, up the stairs, into his apartment.

His bedroom was dark, and I stumbled around, bumped into the dresser, giggled, flopped on the bed, and flung my shoes across the room. He sat down next to me and we continued kissing. I wiggled out of my shirt, unclasped my bra, and he asked, "What are you doing?"

I kissed him harder. "Give me your hand," I instructed. He listened, felt around, kind of gently at first, and then played with the string of my thong.

"Wait," he said. Then, in a whisper, "I've never done this before."

And a light bulb went on; everything clicked. I thought, *he's just nervous is all*. No problem! I'm a great teacher! It would be a Hemingway moment. Full of testosterone-like, animalistic conduct. If only I had a penis! I was drunk, thrilled, and as giddy as I'd been when I lost my V-card at seventeen—on the damp basement floor at a friend's house.

I straddled his legs and pushed him back on the bed, unbuttoned his shirt, pressed my lips against his chest. I undressed him down to his underwear and noticed he was wearing briefs. For a moment, I wanted to tell him that boxers are much sexier. I imagined myself buying him a pair for our one-month anniversary. They'd be red and silky, decorated in little white hearts. I licked the palm of my hand and reached for him, but he got up, leaving me puddled on the bed.

"Hold on," he said. "We need music."

My God, I thought. *Could he be any cuter? He wants music for his first time. He wants the fairy tale, too.* I watched him flip through his CD collection, put something in the player, and come back to bed.

He became assertive, ripped off my panties, hands rubbed all over my body. His fingers penetrated me, and I remember throwing my head back, very dramatically, and letting some porn-like whimper slip out.

And then, the music came on.

"Willkommen, bienvenue, welcome. Im Cabaret, au Cabaret, to Cabaret." And Joel proceeded to finger me, haphazardly, while singing along, as if he were auditioning for a part in my favorite musical.

It was when Joel belted out, "You can tell my Papa, that's all right. Because he comes in here, every night. But don't tell Mama what you saw," sounding like, and sadly resembling, Liza Minnelli, that the love balloon popped.

I told him I had a stomachache, could feel a cold coming on, that I'd left the oven on, anything to make a quick exit. He didn't put up a fight. Instead he helped collect my belongings and called me a cab. It was moot to ask the million-dollar question—I knew the answer, and if he was unsure prior to the evening, he certainly wasn't by the end of it.

That day in the hair salon turned out to be disastrous, too. The goop the stylist applied to my head smelled like rotten eggs and burned my scalp. The intended spiral curls that were supposed to change my life looked like a bad crimp job—think Cyndi Lauper circa 1986. I never got another. And like the lousy perm, I never went on another blind date. The ambiguous set-up, nervous meeting, and high expectations only to be let down in the end, is too much for me. Maybe it's fundamental, though. Maybe all girls need an I-Fooled-Around-with-a-Gay-Virgin story to mature, to become unique in our own way. Or maybe we need such a story to get our mothers off our backs, to get them to stop fixing us up.

A year later my mother heard through the south Jersey Jewish grapevine, that Joel had officially come out of the closet, that he was happy, working as an engineer and living with a Jewish medical resident somewhere in Philly.

"Why can't *you* find a nice, Jewish doctor," my mother screamed into the phone. "He found one, for God's sake. How hard can it be? You want me to look for you?"

Luckily, my mother doesn't know anyone within a four hundred mile radius of Tallahassee.

What Was She Thinking?

Jennifer Ludovici

About the time I turned twenty-six, my mother became frantic about my unattached state. I was not following the timeline that I'd been groomed to follow: graduate from college, meet a boy, get married, buy a house, have children, live happily ever after. As my thirtieth birthday approached my dad sat down with me and told me that he'd been saving money for my wedding, and I could either continue to save it, or he would give it to me to buy a house.

I bought a house. My mother's panic increased.

It's not that I didn't date, I just never pursued it. I'd had a few serious boyfriends in my life and a few fun flings when I lived overseas, but after my return to the States I'd dated only sporadically. When I reached my thirties, many of my friends had gotten involved in Internet dating. For the most part, they were having a great time going on dates every weekend, only having to suffer through the occasional dud or the even more occasional "get me out of here, this guy's a disaster" encounter. I never came around to it, though, and preferred to get together with my girls for cocktails and hear their war stories rather than create battle scenes of my own.

I think my mom had always dreamt her daughters would marry young and reproduce often. To her credit, she didn't pressure us much in our early twenties, having high hopes that things would occur naturally without her help. To indulge her artistic side, and pass the time as she waited for her own daughters to have their own "special day," she began a career as a flower coordinator for weddings. Growing up I was surrounded by flowers, talk of the perfect bridal bouquet and what centerpiece would make guests stop in their tracks. My mother was surrounded by flowers as well, and lamented the fact that the bridal bouquets were always for someone else's daughter.

When my sister eloped with a man who had two children from a previous marriage and no plans for a second family, she left me holding the bag not only to have a big ceremony, but to provide grandchildren. Somewhere, deep down inside, this caused a tiny crack to occur in my mother's composure . . . just the littlest shadow of panic . . . what if, my mother worried, I didn't come through on the dream?

On my thirty-first birthday, with no dates in site, my mother said to me, "It's not for me, you understand. It's for your father. He *really* wants grandchildren." She started pointing out waiters in restaurants she thought were cute.

When I said no to all of her not-so-discerning-creative suggestions, she decided it was time to get more actively involved. While socializing with friends from her book club, which is an all-married, all-female group ranging in age from thirty to seventy, the topic of unattached relatives came up. Quickly the matchmaking began. Each put their sadly single person out to the group to be pitied, and then paired up by the rest. I can only guess as to how that process was organized, but I can tell you that they put a lot more emphasis on geographic proximity than any other consideration. Age differences? Ignored. Common interests? Not considered. But when one of her cronies threw out the single brother who lives in Richmond, my mother jumped on it.

I was unaware she'd made these arrangements for me, so when out of the blue I got a phone call from a man I'd never met before, I was hesitant. I've never been particularly talented when it comes to gleaning information about a person from their voice, and this occasion was no different. He was polite, which was good, and his voice sounded soft and nonthreatening . . . but he also seemed a little dogged, like given his druthers he wouldn't be on the phone with me any more than I would be on the phone with him, which, unfortunately, I took as a good sign. He explained to me that his sister and my mother were in a book club together. His sister had given him my number and he wanted to know if we could meet for a drink. Knowing that my mother's book club ran the gamut in age ranges, my assumption was that one of the younger members had suggested we get together. He had an old Richmond accent that reeked of the old boy network and scotch, but lots of young Richmonders were affecting the same drawl, so it was hard to tell what exactly I was dealing with. I quickly ran down a list of options in my head, but panicked on the spot and heard myself say, "of course." We decided to meet at Metro, my local haunt, a restaurant about a block and a half away from my house.

I immediately called my mom and told her I'd received this strange call and asked her to please fill me in. She told me her friend said her brother was fun loving and single, so she thought, why not? I explained, again, that I really didn't need any help dating and that I was very happy with my current life. I asked if she'd ever met the brother before and she said she hadn't, but that the sister is so cool and fun that she was sure the brother would be a wonderful person and we would have a brilliant time. Since I'd already agreed to meet him, I conceded, one drink wouldn't hurt.

A few days later I went through the ritual of fixing my hair and putting on lipstick, embarrassed that I was hoping to impress this guy, and headed up the street to Metro.

Metro is a cozy place, the absolute epitome of a neighborhood spot complete with bartenders who not only know your name but know your favorite drink. At happy hour on a busy day, there are usually no more than twenty people there. I walked in, and in a quick glance around the room figured I'd gotten there first. There was a group of four or five guys at one end of the bar and a couple at the other, and an old guy having a beer in a booth. Cursing myself for my penchant for punctuality I took a seat, ordered a martini and started chatting with the utterly adorable bartender.

Typically my girlfriends and I go in for drinks and dinner, and it was unusual that I was hanging out at the bar alone. The cutie bartender brought me my drink and asked me where my posse was. Sadly, I told him, I was flying solo that evening. I hesitated a bit and said, "Actually, I'm meeting a date."

He raised an eyebrow. "Really? Like a blind date?" he asked.

Embarrassed I confessed the story.

"So, you've never met him before?" he asked.

I started to panic. "No. Otherwise they would call it something other than a blind date, right?"

He lifted his arm and discretely pointed behind me. "Um . . . that guy's meeting someone, too."

I turned and made eye contact with the guy in the booth. He mouthed my name, and I swear, my heart sank. While I don't know the exact age of my date, my guess is he was between sixty and sixty-five years old.

I turned back to the bartender briefly and said, "Now that's a surprise." He laughed, poured the remainder of the martini shaker into my glass, and with a wink and an amused lilt to his voice said, "Have fun."

I started to think all the positive thoughts I could. He wasn't an ugly man, and he did still have most of his hair. He stood to shake my hand as I came over to the table and I noted the nice blue eyes, considered that gray has been described as distinguished, and that sadly, he looked like a really sweet grandfather who spent his evenings with his slippers on reading by the fire. No, I told myself, focus on only the positives. A plus, I thought, his sweater isn't hideous! It was just a plain navy blue Ralph Lauren and not some horrid Bill Cosby sweater from the eighties that some older gentlemen have a taste for. But he had the belly of an older man, and as I leaned in for the introductory kiss on the cheek I definitely got a whiff of old man smell. Then again, maybe that was just his cologne. If it is his cologne, I wondered, does that count as a positive?

I could tell from his expression that he, too, had expected someone a little more age appropriate for him. Though he was smiling, there was something about it that was a bit sad, or maybe it was his eyes that gave away his disappointment. We had both been duped, and now we had at least one uncomfortable hour to spend with each other before we could call our respective matchmakers and give them a good talking to.

The waitress came to the table and asked if we would like anything. My martini was still swilling over the edges of the glass and his beer was empty, so he ordered drink, looked at me, and smiled. The conversation started awkwardly as we searched for common ground. We started down the list of standard questions.

"Do you have brothers or sisters?" he asked.

I told him about my older sister who also lived in Richmond.

"What about you?" I asked.

He had a sister. We were off to a roaring start.

A ten-second silence followed as we sipped our drinks, both of us knowing that the conversation was dangerously close to a complete halt. In order to avoid the looming uncomfortable silence I pulled out the most inane question from my bag of tricks: "Do you have pets?" As it turned out, we both had cats. Not an interesting topic, but considering our lack of options we went with it. After discussing the problem of shedding cat hair, being able to leave cats at home during weekend vacations, vet bills, and the pros and cons of feline dentistry we'd exhausted the subject. On the upside, a good twenty minutes had passed and both our drinks were half gone.

Tapping my nervous foot and drawing a blank on anything of interest to talk about, I fell back on another good small talk topic. I told him I'd just finished renovating my house, which, in the historic district where we lived, usually hits on some common ground. Thankfully, that gave us another bit of conversation to smile through, as he asked about sanding floors and I told him about discovering plywood under the bathroom carpet. He laughed and commented that it could have been much worse, and again, the conversation sputtered to an end.

He launched into his home renovation tale while I nodded and interjected appropriate questions. Did he do the sanding himself? He'd hired it out. Did he have to deal with the old wiring? Yes, but his electrician was brilliant. I looked at my drink, not much more to go. I was no longer focusing on what to say but how to make this horribly awkward date end.

I finished up my martini and decided that if I didn't order another drink he would get the cue and we could be put out of our misery. To my delight, he was a socially competent man. He finished his beer before the waitress could return, and with a, "Well?" and a slap of his hands on his knees we were done. The waitress brought our bill and after the typical dance about whether or not I could contribute, he told me it had been his pleasure, slid some bills in the book and stood up. We walked together to the front door. I turned to my cute and smirking bartender and waved goodbye, and we walked out the door. He thanked me for meeting him, I wished him well and we headed in opposite directions down the street. As soon as I'd turned the corner to head home, I whipped out my phone and called my mom.

I was furious, yet she was absolutely doubled over with laughter. "Really, Jen," she said, "it was only one drink! Had it really done any harm?"

I'm not sure she understood that while no harm was done, I had been embarrassed that I'd been sent on a date with someone who was not "old enough to be my father," but literally *as old as* my father! And what was worse, he had been just as embarrassed to have been set up with me. At that moment, she was banned from ever medaling with my love life again. And to her credit, she never did.

A year later, without any assistance, I met the man who would be my husband. Ironically, he is four years younger than me. My mother adores him. Ultimately she admitted that mothers do not always know best, and she's glad she only ventured once into actively meddling with my love life. In the end, matchmaking was simply not her calling.

Howie the Putz

Eve Lederman

I grew up in an Orthodox house in which the worst offense was not to get pregnant or use drugs; those things were impossibilities in the realm of alien abduction . . . no, the worst thing was to accidentally use the meat silverware for dairy. My mother would have a seizure if you mistakenly used the wrong utensil and she'd make a mad dash to the backyard to immediately bury the wayward fork in dirt where it would stay for the next twelve months until it cleansed itself back to its kosher state. I was the only kid on the block with a graveyard of knives instead of departed pets behind the house.

My mother and I are fundamentally different: She likes gefilte fish. I like premarital sex. She believes you shouldn't call a man, or beat him at a game of Scrabble or ping pong. "Wait for him to find you; turn your sunny face to the window and he will magically appear like the jingle of an ice cream truck," she once said. I think if you're stuck at the top of the Coney Island Ferris wheel with your date, you happen to be wearing skirt and the cart is already rocking . . . why not indulge in some amusement?

My mother wants me to marry a nice, Jewish doctorlawyer-accountant, with the emphasis on Jewish. If I married a farm animal she probably wouldn't mind as long as it was kosher. She fulfilled her mother's dream by marrying a doctor at age twenty-two, but she settled for bitterness instead of risking happiness. Her face, puckered and dour, often looks like she just exited an airplane latrine. Her life is pallid and practical, flat and gray. She has never traveled alone, nor paid her own rent. And her marriage—ordered primarily around feeding my father—is not one I wish to emulate.

Oddly, it was always my father who set me up on dates. There would be a new boy waiting for me whenever I came home from college for a holiday, magically appearing to tempt me like the Golden Calf at Sabbath lunch. First was an AHL hockey player who had more teeth than brain cells. I recall my father asking, as an icebreaker, if he had any siblings. "Siblings?" Jeff responded quizzically, cocking his head as if he'd been asked to rework the theory of relativity. "Brothers or sisters?" I added. "Ohhh, those," he responded with a look of relief. "Yeah, I got two."

I gave up on my father, and my mother immediately picked up the slack, passing my number out like hard candy to any woman in line at the kosher bakery. It wasn't long before she phoned to tell me that she had given my number to Howie through his mother, an acquaintance of hers in the Jewish community. She had no idea what he looked like and I kept pressing her to find out if he was bald. I have trouble saying "no" to bald men. They've been rejected by their own hair—how can I possibly add another blow to their receding self-esteem? I agree to dinner and some fooling around, and I keep my revulsion to myself.

My mother had, however, intensively reviewed his résumé: Howie began in mergers and acquisitions with an investment banking firm before making a lateral move into corporate financing with a top-tier New York law firm. The only other thing I knew was that Howie's brother Stan was in my grammar school class; he used to pull his arms in close to his chest and flap his hands like a baby bird whenever he got overexcited. Stan was also in my high school band; I never gave him a second look since he played the oboe and anyone who puffs their cheeks out like that is just queer. Needless to say, I didn't have high hopes for Howie when he phoned a week later.

"Hi, uh, this is Howie. My mother gave me your phone number."

So he's just trying to please his mother? I saw a twenty-year storyboard unfold in which he danced around his demanding, domineering mother, traveling upstate on weekends to help her mend a patch in the screen door or clean out the fridge. Her exacting ways having beaten him into passivity, I'd resent his neediness and he'd forever seek out unconditional affection from me to fill the void of maternal love. He probably suffered from constipation, a symptom of all her withholding. . . . Lulled by my psychoanalytic reverie, I gave in to his dull chatter, and, bored into submission, let him choose a restaurant in my neighborhood.

A few nights later, Howie showed up. He had hair, lots of it. It curled, it spiraled, it danced a jig. And underneath all that hair was what appeared to be a twelve-year-old boy. "Does your mommy know you're here all by yourself?" I wanted to say. He was too skinny, and though he was a runner, I was hoping for a sprinter—the guys with watermelon thighs.

Leaving my building, I instinctively turned left to cross First Avenue, thinking he was taking me to Lexington or

Madison—show me the town. Instead Howie guided me to the right. I shot him a quizzical look. To the right was York, the armpit of the city. There's a hospital and a store that rents vacuums. But Howie had managed to find a little Italian place, dark, grim, and full of middle-aged couples with middle-management desk jobs. I felt like I should be wearing sensible shoes. Our conversation was rational and levelheaded. He talked in bullet points, giving me the memo version of his life, but there was something comforting about his organization and the banality of it all. I didn't have to impress him with wit or charm, and I could tell that if we were together, he'd never forget an anniversary or the dry cleaning.

At the two-hour mark he informed me he'd pretty much covered everything about his life as a lawyer, and by the time his fruit arrived, the conversation was at a lull. I took a bite of strawberry . . . and suddenly a mouse darted in front of us; I completely freaked out. Howie, however, said nonchalantly, "Oh, I don't really mind mice. It's their fecal matter that bothers me."

I was stunned. I have never actually heard anyone use the word "fecal" on a first date. But then I realized, hey, this qualifies as bathroom humor . . . I could get along with this guy. I shared farting jokes and decided I might be able to bring this boy home after all.

And Howie was a good listener. I talked about scraping for work as a writer and the grind of being a freelancer, which I hoped would squelch any ideas he might have about splitting the check. Turns out, I didn't even have to do the fake bend toward my purse when it came. I was so elated that I agreed to another outing the next weekend, this time at a sports bar on the West Side.

On date two I biked across town for what will forever be called "The Salad Dressing Incident." We ate at the bar, my back slightly toward him to watch the basketball game on TV. As we're eating, I detect a spitting noise from over my shoulder, and out of the corner of my eye I see Howie swishing some of his Caesar salad around in his mouth and spitting out the excess dressing into a glass, now full of green, swampy muck.

I was repulsed into silence, turned away, and focused intently on the TV. The look on the waiter's face as he took the glass away was priceless. He and I shared a glance, his eyebrows raised as in "what are you doing with this guy"; my shoulders shrugged, implying, "look, I'm in my 30s, the field is thinning and my mother set me up."

To top the night off, there was a little quarrel upon leaving when, around midnight, I mounted my bike to go home.

"You can't bike at this hour," he informed me.

"I'm fine," I said casually. "I'll be home in ten minutes."

"That's really bad judgment," he said angrily. "There are certain things you just don't do in the city." *That's right,* I wanted to yell. *Like slosh food around in your mouth and regurgitate it into a glass.*

But I let it go because I was excited—not by him, but by the prospect of being able to bring a guy home and not have to lie about his Jewish status, which had been a tough sell with my last boyfriend, Mike Guidarelli. He had arms that looked like big hams; everything about him screamed pork.

And then, unexpectedly, Howie leaned in to me and whispered, "I can smell you all the time." Instinctively I leaned toward my armpit, thinking this was a bad thing.

"No. You. I smell *you*. Even when you're not here," he cooed.

Granted, I did have a unique smell at the time, a mixture of Dr. Bonner's peppermint soap and blue ridge wildflower oil. He was, I think, in love with my scent, and in that tender moment, the gruesome salad incident slipped away.

For date three I invited Howie over to my place for brunch, thinking I'd avoid additional public spittoon episodes, and discovered another odd personal habit. While the eggs cooked, Howie yelled to me from the bathroom, asking if I had more toilet paper. I didn't and, embarrassed, said I'd run out for more.

"Don't bother," he shouted back, "Just hand me a piece of the newspaper."

I frantically started combing through the *Times*—I couldn't hand him the Style section with the wedding listings—that would be sacrilege. Metro? No. Business for his "business"? After a five-minute debate and rebuttal on the toilet paper (I won and made the purchase), I was somehow able to put this episode, along with the salad dressing debacle, out of my head and snuggle up to him on the couch by reminding myself that my last decent date needed a green card.

I leaned in for a kiss and casually planted my hand between his legs for a little "meet and greet." I rubbed, I roamed. No signs of life. So I casually moved up to the stomach, retreated to the chest with a little massage, and finished off with a couple pats on the shoulder. He jumped up to get some juice, announced that he had to go in to the office, and ended the afternoon mid-upzip.

But I was not deterred. I've always been a fixer upper. Apartments, shelter dogs. Give me a skinny man and I'll have him on a lifting routine in a week. Looking back now, maybe I had also internalized some of my mother. Perhaps I thought I didn't deserve more; growing up, my school clothes were from Kmart; our generic ice cream had that shoe polish patina; and I got my hair cut at the spinster Cut 'N Curl. This was the man my mother chose for me; perhaps she knew best.

I persisted, but by our sixth date it was utterly clear: His Hebrew National was limp. His matzoh balls had grown cold. We were at his place; I thought with the home toilet advantage he might be more comfortable, and after wolfing down our takeout I threw myself at him. I kneaded it like challah, patted it like a blintz. I danced the Hora around it and recited every blessing I could think of, but to no avail. I could deal with small if it at least had . . . personality, but after an hour I pretty much gave up.

If he had compensated in some other way, I might have softened myself. Whispered sweet retorts in my ear or kissed my *amicus curiae* until I was wild with desire. But no, taking off his tie was the most demonstrative move he made. My court swiftly made its final determination—case dismissed.

Just when I was about to do so, Howie's office uprooted him to Bogotá to prosecute drug lords. Many love letters ensued, begging me to visit him and promising to pick me up in an armored car. Surprisingly, I found that at a distance Howie became ardent, even fervent in his attraction me.

"Dear Eve," he wrote. "I am beguiled by you, your mystery and depth. You thrill me. I see a woman whose beauty is animated by her spirit. I respect your vision and insight and I am moved by what you do. I am turned on by you. You are, simply put, enchanting."

Hmm . . . suddenly *I* was wooed. Could I just date the man by mail? Why didn't he show me this side of him before?

I realized, though, that I was in love with the idea of being in a relationship that my mother would love. I was staying with Howie to make my mother happy. I have never tried to make my mother happy. Why was I starting now?

So I stopped. Ended it with Howie and never looked back . . . until seven years later. Still single, I Googled him on a whim. He was back from Bogotá, and had given up pursuing drug cartels in favor of a quiet life, heading up a company that makes accounting software. Online I read an anecdote he told at a conference about an auditor that failed to complete a compliance review. Suddenly I had a vision of him coming home to me in Connecticut, plopping his briefcase on the table, and saying, "Honey, the funniest thing happened today with our automation software. . . ." According to his Web site, he's grown the business into a multi-million dollar enterprise; but I also saw his picture. . . and he's gone completely bald.

Meeting Morty—Or,

How My Mother's Friend's Friend's Daughter's Friend's Brother Became My Favorite Ex-Boyfriend

Rachel Sklar

My mom is one of the sweetest women I know—which makes her almost impervious to the harsh realities of the dog-eat-dog world of dating. For her, phrases like "give him a chance, you never know" and "the worst that happens, you make a new friend" are blithely uttered about men she's never seen, knows nothing about, and who most likely have zero compatibility with her darling daughter. Well, except for being Jewish. It was that ineffable qualifier that prompted her—without a second thought—to give my number to her friend Natalie for her friend Sheila so her daughter Cathy could pass it on to her friend Marcy for her brother, Morty.

My mom didn't get why I was annoyed. "You gave out my number?" quickly escalated to "You gave out my number to a guy named *Morty*?" What did he look like? How old was he? What did he do? Mom didn't know; it had never occurred to her to ask. Why would it? Morty was Natalie's friend's daughter's friend's brother. Why wouldn't I want to meet him?

I have been on few blind dates, mostly because I quickly discovered that "Jewish" and "single" were pretty much the only criteria being applied, resulting in the disquieting realization that my friends obviously found me less attractive than I'd thought. But with my mom, it was different: This came from out of the blue, from a woman who, though she had never previously betrayed any anxiety about my dating life, probably should have been a bit more interested in the qualities a future son-in-law brought to the table.

"Morty" quickly became "Morty, the Short Balding Accountant," because, after all, my mom couldn't disprove it. (It was at this point that she said, "the worst that happens, you make a new friend" to which I, a beleaguered junior lawyer at a soul-sapping Manhattan law firm, snapped, "I don't even have time to see the friends I have!") Still, she must have sensed my flexibility on that point, seeing as the bar for "new friend" had recently been satisfied by a guy I'd agreed to meet for dinner based on the fact that he'd seen me on a plane and eavesdropped enough information to get my phone number through my law school alumni office. If Plane Stalker could get the nod, I guess I could make time for Morty, who may or may not have been a short, balding accountant. Besides, now it wasn't just about me, or my mom—now my actions had consequences for Natalie, Sheila, Cathy, and Marcy, too. For the sake of them, I figured it couldn't hurt. I awaited his call.

And awaited, and awaited—what, this Morty was too busy to pick up a phone?

A week went by, then two; thoughts of Morty were lost in piles of due diligence binders and all-nighters fueled by Diet Coke and take-out. In fact, I was so close to the edge that when a long weekend suddenly opened up I impulsively decided to take an impromptu trip, just buy a ticket and get the hell out of Dodge.

I was trolling Expedia, deciding between Palm Springs (where my Canadian parents flee every winter) and Sweden (where I used to live) when the phone rang.

"This is Rachel," I said, in my best lawyer voice.

"Hi, this is Morty," he said, snapping me back from daydreams of strapping blond Nordic men. Swedes are very attractive. "So, you're Cathy's friend?"

As it happens, I was not Cathy's friend; the last time I'd seen Cathy was in 1987 at summer camp, where she was the drama counselor. I remembered her yelling at me once during rehearsal when I ran offstage mid-scene because someone had walked in with a pizza. Was Morty was under the erroneous impression that someone in that crazy set-up chain actually *knew* me? Yikes. Maybe he didn't actually *know* that he was calling his sister's friend's mom's friend's friend's daughter. If so, he was already one up on me.

I explained the connection. Awkward silence. Somewhere in there floated the silent acknowledgment that our families thought we were really big losers. Change of subject. "So, you're working late." (It was 9:00 P.M.) "What are you still doing at the office?" Only now does it strike me that he thought he'd be able to just leave a message.

"I'm deciding where I should go tomorrow," I said. (It was Thursday.) "What do you think, Palm Springs or Sweden?"

There was a moment of silence, and then Morty made the mistake of asking me to elaborate, listening politely as I launched into particulars . . . and kept going. Somewhere during my near-monologue I remember thinking that, wow, Morty the Accountant seemed cool; I wish I could remember the three words he got in edgewise to give me that impression. I found out later that he called his sister immediately after and told her never to give his number out again.

I didn't know that, of course, so when I returned from Palm Springs (advantage: sunshine) I called him, and we agreed to meet. He offered to pick me up from my building (classy), where I made him wait in the lobby while I frantically tried on outfits (less classy). Maybe my mom was right, I clearly needed help.

As I rode down in the elevator, I felt that familiar bubble of pre–blind date excitement building, equal parts hope and possibility right before you meet someone, when they could still be anyone, including someone great. But over ten floors, I steeled myself: He seemed nice, sure, but the odds were slim that he'd be cute.

I stepped out of the elevator. There was a guy sitting patiently on the couch, waiting. He stood up and smiled, hand out. I shook it, saying hi, but inside my head I was yelling things like *He's cute! He's tall! He has hair!* After all that, Morty was a *babe*!

We stood there, smiles more genuine, possibly out of relief. "I was thinking we could go to the Hudson," he said as we walked out, sounding pleased with himself. The Hudson Hotel had opened less than two months before, and it was the current hot-spot *du jour*, complete with the obligatory celebrities and models. Great date place—if you were a celebrity or a model.

"Don't you think we'll have trouble getting in?" I asked, brow a-furrow. Morty looked at me with faint annoyance.

"I think it'll be fine," he said, with the air of someone who had been many times. Our first power struggle. *Fine, get kicked out of your fancy bar, hotshot*, I thought. Sometimes I am competitive.

We walked over and sure enough, there was a line, and the snippy guy with the clipboard told us that they were "at capacity." I willed my face not to look smug; the look on his face suggested that I did not quite succeed. And so we were left with a slightly strained silence and the awkwardness of finding somewhere else to go. First dates should never include travel time.

But travel we did, hailing a cab downtown, trying to drum up a destination. We finally settled on Fez (my suggestion), a flickery, middle-eastern lounge with low couches and swingy, beaded curtains. We sat down, ordered drinks, and, finally, started hitting it off—especially since he'd arranged to have food put in front of me and I'd pointed out that the girl at the bar was totally showing her thong.

More drinks were ordered. My smile became a tad goofy. Hi Morty! You're fun! He was smiling too. I got chatty. Did he know that I was really a writer? That I'd written a book during law school? That I'd recorded a pop song while I was in Sweden? That my sister was visiting because it was my birthday? It was my birthday! It's true, I had turned twenty-eight somewhere between the thong and the third drink, and I proudly informed Morty that the *real* party was tomorrow at some bar in Soho. Our names were on a *list*. Morty, that denizen of the Hudson, seemed suitably impressed. Then he whipped out his phone and found my book on Amazon, showing off his pre-Blackberry technology. It was the year 2000, and now *I* was impressed. Morty was *cool!* And cute. Hi Morty!

Suddenly, the waitress appeared—with cake, and a candle. I looked at Morty. "Happy twenty-eighth, birthday girl," he said, grinning, as my heart did a little flip.

We ended up at a diner at 4 A.M., convulsed in laughter and not even because we were drunk. It was 5 A.M. when we caught a cab back uptown, and between the cake and the company I was ready for the kiss. Open body language, the artful tilt of the head, city block after city block—nothing. That Morty may not have been choosy about his blind dates, but he knew what he was doing.

The next day I got an e-mail wishing me a happy birthday, and a phone call later to say it in person. On Monday he e-mailed to make a plan:

```
To: Morty
From: Rachel
My mom's been busy on my behalf—I'm seeing
Shlomo Feingold tonight and Seymour Hirschenbaum
tomorrow.
```

```
To: Rachel
From: Morty
A hundred bucks says Shlomo and Seymour don't get
in a combined twenty-five words of conversation.
```

I was no longer drunk, and Morty was still funny. A good sign! My heart did that little flip again. Or maybe it was my stomach—Morty had fed me well.

I consider it emblematic of our relationship that on our second date we saw *Dude, Where's My Car?* We were giggling as we left the theatre, still high on dumb humor and sitting next to each other in the dark for ninety minutes. I seriously almost grabbed him right there, but we had the good manners to wait until we got to a Champagne bar, where he ordered up a bottle. I would have settled for a Diet Coke. Is there anything better than the googly-eyed look on someone's face just before they kiss you for the first time? I can still remember. Champagne and butterflies. There's nothing better.

I feel a little guilty leading you on like this since I know how it ended, namely three-and-a-half months later with me whipping a beanie baby across his apartment. (Drama!) And even though I know it's for the best, we're better as friends, etc., etc., etc., it does make me sort of sad as I relive it in my head, and now on paper. My mom was so proud of herself. As she should have been—she had set me up with a terrific, terrific guy, however inadvertently. But "terrific" doesn't necessarily mean "right"—and when it's not right, it has to end at some point. So, on we go.

I can still remember sitting on the counter in his kitchen as he put our Chinese takeout on plates (so fancy!), looking at me and saying, "For the record: beautiful eyes." I can remember him so proud of himself because he'd looked up my name on Napster and found a song called "Slut Named Rachel." I can remember sending him e-mails with subject lines like "Everything's Coming Up Morty!" More than anything, I can remember the laughter—doubled-over, can't-breathe, stomach-hurting laughter that flared up over e-mail, on the phone, and frequently in bed, though now that I think of it my occasional habit of cracking up uncontrollably may have ruined the mood a few times.

Recently I found an old e-mail, "Top Ten Reasons Why I Haven't Heard from Morty the Day Before Valentine's Day," an excuse to make fun of his near-obsessive fastidiousness ("#7—You accidentally touched the pole in the subway and are still washing your hands furiously"). That was a joke, like my Valentine's Day gift: the full "Slut Named Rachel" CD, special-ordered. At that time we were at the midpoint of the relationship, but it had all gone at warp speed: By the first few weeks we felt like we'd been together forever and by the first few months we were already acting like it. Comfortable, yes, but not exactly . . . hot.

And so . . . beanie baby. It wasn't because he'd done anything bad—he didn't cheat, he wasn't mean to me, he kept me well fed. I would almost have preferred that, to have something to blame. The truth was far worse: He just didn't feel the same way I did. (How's this for shorthand: I said something like, "You make me melt," and he got all quiet. Ouch.) Everything about us that was so great—the laughing, the goofy hijinks, the private jokes—well, it just wasn't enough. I railed at him, tearfully; didn't he *know* what he was letting *go*? He knew, that wasn't the problem. The problem was, he was still doing it.

That part I couldn't blame on my mom, though she tried her best to comfort me when I called her on the phone, hyperventilating. Every hour. On the hour. Yeah, we've all been there. That part sucks.

But the point of this story, really, is about the part that came after; that is to say, why the part that came before—the breakup and the hurt and the puffy eyes and endless playing of sad songs—was worth it. It was the part *before* the before that made the difference. And he knew it, too. On our third date, the one with the Chinese takeout, Morty stopped and said to me, "If this doesn't work out—me and you—can we make sure we stay friends?" He immediately apologized for talking about the end when we were just beginning, but I thought that sounded like an awesome deal, and the best kind of compliment. I agreed, immediately.

A few weeks after we split, I ran into Morty at the airport (seven pounds lighter—thank you, breakup diet!). It was good to see each other, if awkward, and we said we'd be in touch. And, we were. I honestly can't remember when it went from awkward and weird to telling each other about our hilarious dates and trying to set each other up, but it did, and somewhere along the line we *did* stay friends, great friends, the kind who all your friends meet and then want to set up with *their* friends. The kind of friends who have history, and a whole other history piled on top of it.

A few weeks ago, my mom came to town, and I made reservations for a dinner so that she could meet my best friends, Morty included.

She loved him.

How Do You Say "Threesome" in Japanese?

Benita Gold

From the bathroom I could hear her leaving one of her ten-minute messages. My mother's an actress in search of a stage and for her an answering machine is an opportunity to play to an audience.

"Hello my proud beauty! It's your one and only mother. You must be out walking that dog. I hope you don't go into the park after dark. Your father and I had dinner with the Glickmans last night and of course they raved about you and your personality and [with sarcasm] you know how I *hate* that. We went to the Sandbar—love their hard shells. Well you know your shy mother, I started talking to two young men at the next table—Rick and Ron—They are brothers from Cincinnati—well now Rick lives in L.A. and Ron lives in Chicago . . ."

I stared into my closet trying to decide what to wear. When I'm in a hurry I let my mother ramble on and I call her back.

". . . but he'll be in New York on Wednesday and I told him you would love to have dinner with him. He is a very successful, good looking investment banker—"

I grab the phone. "Mom, who *is* this guy?"

"Oh you are there!" Mom exclaimed delighted to hear my voice. Before she can gather more steam I stop her. "I am running late but just tell me fast about the guy."

"We thought Ron was absolutely charming and had a very good sense of humor. It doesn't have to be serious, but he will be in New York and I'm sure he'll take you somewhere nice for dinner. He is a little older than you. I'd say about thirty-eight."

"You said he is handsome." I prod her.

"Well Lol Glickman thought he was handsome. I would say . . . nice looking."

Usually, she is not one of those Jewish mothers who is obsessed with curing my single state. I was twenty-seven and the last time she had fixed me up was ten years before and the guy had been gorgeous. So I took her at her word, and decided it would be okay to trust her matchmaking offerings.

As promised, I had a message from him a few days later.

"Hi Benita, my name is Ron Schaeffer. I met your mother, Rita Ann, in a restaurant in Sarasota—Wow! What a live wire. If you are anything like her, I can't wait to meet you. I love New York restaurants and I'm on an expense account so we will live it up. I'll call you when I get to town on Tuesday."

Ron had a deep, flirtatious DJ voice and listening to his message I started to get a crush on him. Moreover, he had hooked me with the promise of dining out at a top restaurant. When he phoned on Tuesday, we talked about where to dine. I offered up a few suggestions, but he'd said he had a great place in mind. When he insisted on picking me up at my apartment I was charmed and thought "tres old world gentleman." I decided to dress very Audrey in *Breakfast at Tiffany's* which seemed appropriate for an elegant dinner with an out of town businessman.

Since I didn't own a sophisticated, little black dress I had to go shopping. I found a wonderful one—sleeveless, form hugging, high in front and lower in the back with black ribbon criss-crossing my bare back and bought sheer black pantyhose with a flower embroidered at the ankle. I was ready.

When I answered the door I was taken aback. He looked like somebody's uncle. My mother said he was in his thirties, which I envision as still youngish with tousled sandy hair and just the beginnings of crows feet; but this guy was pot bellied, graying, and balding which to me said forty-plus. He was at least twenty pounds overweight and wore a business suit, which shouldn't have been surprising since he was here on business, but I usually dated musicians and actors who only wore suits to funerals or weddings. I like guys that look like Jesus and he looked like President Taft. He lecherously eyeballed my ankles, and I realized he thought the flower on my stocking was a tattoo.

Okay, so I wasn't attracted to him. I was still going to have a fantastic dinner out and was already fantasizing about escargot, lobster bisque, and steak au poivre in a charming, candle-lit boite.

"Where we going?" I ask as he opened the taxi door for me. Love that gentlemanly stuff.

"A Japanese restaurant. Have you ever had sushi?"

I was crestfallen. In my defense, I hasten to explain that I love sushi now but, this was only 1980 and the sushi boom had not yet happened. The only raw fish I had ever tasted was lox. As I was mentally saying goodbye to the French restaurant with the cheese course and the sommelier, I'm sure my face conveyed my disappointment.

"You will love it," Ron said flatly, obviously not caring.

The taxi dropped us off at a sterile restaurant in the East 50s. When we walked in, Ron shooed the host's offer of a table and led me to the sushi bar. Again I was disappointed as I had not dressed up to sit at a counter. As I struggled onto the high stool I caught Ron staring as my already short dress rode up my thigh. I tried to tug the hem toward my knees but it was too tight to move much.

The other customers were all Japanese. *Who else would eat Japanese food?* I thought. Ron spoke a few words in Japanese to the sushi chef and looked at me to see the affect it was having. While I could see he was showing off, which I thought was kind of touching as he was practically old enough to be my dad, I was nonetheless impressed. I started to get the excited feeling I get when I am traveling and thrown into a foreign culture.

"I feel like I am in another country which is my favorite way to feel," I rhapsodized.

Ron didn't respond, he only nodded at me, and then, without consulting me, ordered a series of increasingly inexplicable items. Each course placed in front of us contained a strange series of edibles garnished with seaweed. I tried everything and liked none of it, but I was enjoying the exotic experience.

Ron inhaled his food and didn't seem concerned that I barely ate. He was however very concerned with how much I drank and refilled my glass of hot, sweet wine after every sip. While I didn't like the taste, I embraced it as part of this new experience and it did leave a nice afterglow.

"This place is the closest I've been able to find to my favorite sushi bar in Kyoto." Ron told me.

"Have you traveled a lot in Japan?" I asked quite unnecessarily as he was launching into a ten-minute travelogue. I started to get nervous he was going to pull out a projector and slides.

"Why did you learn Japanese?" I interjected, trying to add something to the conversation.

"I've traveled there a few times and I think it's important to be able to talk to the natives when you are in a country."

"Me too!" I agreed adamantly. "I spent my sophomore year in Rome and I was always embarrassed by the American tourists who expected everything to be just like home. Why travel?"

He looked at me, smiled tolerantly then continued to talk about Japan.

"So tell me about your meeting with my mom and how she managed to get you to call me." I asked switching gears to a subject that was more entertaining to me.

"Your mom is quite a character." Ron enthused. "My brother and I couldn't stop talking about her."

"Neither can me and my therapist," I quipped and he laughed. Not exactly the bantering my mother led me to expect, but at least a good audience.

As we walked out of the restaurant, Ron said "I know a club right down the block. Do you want to go have a drink?"

"Sure."

We walked to the next doorway and he announced, "This is it."

We stepped down three stairs into a tiny, dimly lit room with a small bar and four tables. There was a Japanese bartender and a Japanese waitress in a kimono.

Boy he really likes Japanese stuff, I thought.

We were seated in the corner at the only banquette. Our waitress—a pretty young Japanese woman came over to the table and asked Ron if he kept a bottle there.

"I've got a bottle of scotch. Bring two glasses, please."

"Actually I'd like a glass of champagne." I said, noticing that once again Ron had not considered what I would like.

"They only serve by the bottle." Ron said dismissively. His manner irritated me.

"Fine. I'll have a bottle."

The waitress walked two inches over to the manager who was leaning on the bar to repeat my request and then she returned to our table and sat down between me and my date. I was stunned and getting a creepy feeling. Was she a geisha? Ron didn't look surprised that she'd joined us. I was unsure of the protocol so initiated a stilted conversation.

"Your kimono is beautiful," I offered lamely.

"Thank you. Your dress is beautiful too." she replied sweetly.

I stared into her face trying to see under the thick make up for a sign of what she was thinking. I was unsure what was going on and hoped woman to woman she would see this and help me out.

"I love Kabuki theater," I offered, never having seen any.

She looked taken aback.

"I love *Fiddler on the Roof*," she retorted.

Ron added nothing to this cultural exchange, but was smirking at both of us. He looked pleased with himself.

The manager came over with a bottle of champagne. "Would you like to drink this here?"

Ron turned to me with a questioning look.

"Well where else would we have it?" I laughed.

"You come to back room?" the waitress asked me stroking my arm. Clearly, I was in over my head. I wanted out. I thought of my parents who represented safety and protection to me and then remembered they had hooked me up with this pervert in the first place.

I studied Ron's jowly face. It seemed unlikely that a guy would befriend an older couple in Florida and then take their daughter to a sex club. I glanced around the tiny room for telltale signs. The only other customers were a pair of middle-aged Western businessmen who returned my glance and then continued quietly talking. I tried to read their facial expressions for clues.

"What is in the back room?" I asked Ron.

"Very nice. More private," the manager explained.

"We will have more room in the back," the waitress added.

I was trying to figure out what we would need more room for—maybe we were going to toss a Frisbee. "I have enough room. Thanks though," I replied.

Everyone looked at me like I was being difficult or unfriendly.

"Lots of ladies go in the back," the manager reassured me.

Sure, they are all making out with Japanese women to turn on their pot bellied dates, I thought to myself.

"You'll like it" the waitress or hostess or geisha or whatever she was told me.

"Ron, can I talk to you alone?" I asked.

The waitress and manager walked away to give us privacy and stood at the opposite end of the room four inches away.

"Ron, what is with the back room? Is it some kind of orgy den?"

"It is whatever we want it to be. I think we could have a lot of fun and you don't have to do anything you are not comfortable with." He raised an eyebrow and leered at me like I was the last piece of fat belly tuna.

I silently weighed my curiosity and the potential anecdote material against my strong desire to go home. My story of the evening seemed incomplete without knowing what was back there. Maybe there was a hot tub full of "swingers." But I was nervous I might not be able to eyeball the scene and then leave. The evening had taken on such a surreal feel that I wondered if there were women who went in and didn't come out.

Ron leaned in to me, brushing my arm and whispered in my ear in what he probably considered his seducer voice "You are too beautiful to be so uptight." I edged away afraid he might try to lick my ear or blow in it. He sidled closer to me on the banquette and stroked my thigh. "I would love to have the opportunity to satisfy you."

That made my decision easy.

"I am going home," I said, pulling away and getting up from the table. Damn, where was my coat?

"I will take you home." Ron offered switching back to his gentleman mode.

At this point I was eager to be rid of him. "I'd rather go by myself."

With one step I reached the manager behind the bar. "I want my coat please." I grabbed it and rushed out the door. Ron followed and we stood in silence as he hailed a cab then handed me a $20 bill.

"Can I ask you why you thought I'd want to go in the back room?" I asked through the cab's open window.

Ron shrugged. "Well, your mother said you were a wild woman."

Ah hah! Now, my mother and I go way back, so I speak Mom fluently and know she was simply trying to convey that I was a lot of fun, but had inadvertently promised this guy I was a big ho.

"My mother said you were handsome, young, and funny. I guess she was wrong about a lot of things." As we drove off I watched Ron get smaller and smaller until he disappeared.

I Am Not a Gift

Heather Robinson

My brothers and I call our mother, whose real name is Judith, "the Pittsburgh Dazzler," because she exudes an aura of old-fashioned glamour that isn't found on every corner of our hometown. In a city where watching the Steelers play on Sundays—on television—is the highpoint of the week for many, the Dazz—as her nickname has evolved—conducts poetry salons and humanitarian fundraisers in her elegantly appointed townhouse, located a few blocks from Carnegie-Mellon University. She also teaches poetry classes to retirees, most of whom are unrequitedly in love with her. Having been the beauty of Pittsburgh's Taylor Allderdice High School class of '59, back when dating college boys was a mark of status, she still enjoys the attentions of men older than herself and fails to see anything unconventional about a few years' age difference. Never a slave to fashion, she's nonetheless always elegant, whether she is wearing Chanel to the symphony or picking basil in sweats with her three-year-old grandson in the neat herb and flower garden she cultivates alongside her patio.

A social butterfly, the Dazz has long despaired that, in the social realm, her three reclusive children take after our late father. In fact, some of my parents' worst arguments concerned socializing. I remember their more extravagant parties: passed h'or d'oeuvres, the sounds of saxophone and piano drifting through our dining room's open windows and over the pool, its water glowing purple, blue, and gold from overhead lights.

The Dazz loved those parties, mostly because she's a people person. She believes that having lots of friends and activities—including dates (she and my father eventually divorced)—provides inoculation against life's inevitable heartbreaks and disappointments.

Thus when we were growing up, she viewed any sign of her kids' reluctance to socialize with the dread one might expect of a parent perceiving early signs of mental retardation.

"What do you mean you don't want to go to camp?" she would gasp. *"What will you do with yourself?"*

When I was eleven, she broached the subject of my getting contact lenses, saying, "You're pretty, but because you wear glasses, some people might not be able to tell that right away. Don't you want boys to ask you on dates?"

While the Dazz has by now given up the notion that I will ever be a socialite, nothing upends her quite like the sight of me alone at my computer on a weekend night when I'm visiting. If she has a date—and most of the time that's the case—she tries to convince me to tag along.

If nudging me to accompany her on her dates was the extent of her efforts to turn me into a people person, that would be one thing. But I always get the feeling she doesn't view a single woman in her thirties, especially one who has never been married, as quite normal. And every few months she calls to tell me, as if we've never had this conversation before, that she met up with some wonderful old friends and they have a fabulous son.

My mother has many talents, but matchmaking is not one of them. The first time she fixed me up I was only twenty. His name was Barnett Schwartz. He was divorced and in his thirties, but I was home for the summer, bored, and compulsively sweet in the way that only a formerly chubby girl can be. I was emerging from my first love, and first breakup, with Derek, a tall, skinny engineering student I'd met during my sophomore year at the University of Washington in Seattle. In choosing to attend a West Coast school, I'd seen myself as escaping the stifling confines of life—especially social life—in provincial Pittsburgh. Trekking across the beautiful "U-Dub" campus, I had felt moments of pure rapture, and meeting Derek completed the picture. With his chiseled features, sandy stubble, and leather jacket, he set my sheltered Jewish girl's heart a-racing. The English major in me saw him as an archetypal character: rugged and tough but tender, a freethinking, stubborn, iconoclast who came of age in the Great West. All that sex appeal, and he was intellectual, too.

He was my first love, and unfortunately, like most first loves, ours was relatively short-lived. After pressing me all semester for exclusivity, when I agreed to be his alone, he became cold and withdrawn, seemingly overwhelmed—rather like the boy who pleads all year for a puppy and then when the animal actually materializes wants nothing more than to forget about the creature. As year's end approached, I ended it, blaming myself. By the time I arrived home for the summer, I was convinced I'd be lucky to ever have a normal date, much less a normal relationship, again.

No doubt the sight of me sitting around, nursing mild psychosomatic ailments that had developed in the aftermath of my heartbreak, intensified my mother's zeal to see me date. Moreover,

I wasn't getting manicures or shaving my legs. The Dazz probably feared the West Coast had turned me into an anti-social hippie—a fate from which she was determined to save me. Her choice of Barnett had something to do with the fact that the introduction came courtesy of her friend Mona, whom she idolized, rightly enough, for having survived Auschwitz. "It must be ordained in heaven," she told me, "if Mona has okayed the match." When I consented, it was mostly out of fatigue. And maybe a little out of hope.

When Barnett came to my mother's house to pick me up, he rang the bell and entered with a quiet dignity. He wore a suit and tie, though it was a weekend. Standing in our front hall and facing him with my mother by my side, I felt like I was going on a date with a friend's father. My mother had told me Barnett was in his thirties, and although that sounded old to me at the time, I would have guessed that the tall, broad, heavy-set man standing in our front hall was even older—maybe forty. On one hand, my hairline pricked with sweat as I imagined sitting across from him on the date, it was so awkward. But I also got my first inkling of the erotic charge an age difference can produce: In the momentary flash one often gets when encountering a blind date, or any potential partner ("What would it be like to kiss?"), I felt a hint of curiosity.

"Well, Barnett, so wonderful to meet you!" my mother cooed in a delighted, yet formal voice she typically reserved for important business associates of my father's. (At that time, she and my dad were still married).

"Thank you," Barnett said with a nod.

My mother placed her arm on his sleeve and, glancing from Barnett to me and back said, "Well, the two of you look just great. Where do you plan to have lunch?"

"Café Sam," said Barnett.

As they discussed the restaurant, I stepped uneasily from one strappy-sandaled foot to the other (my mother had dressed me for the date in her shoes, as well as a white sweater and psychedelic-looking Pucci skirt from her closet). This was weird. It wasn't that Barnett was so terrible looking—he was about forty pounds overweight, but carried it on a muscular, broad-shouldered build, and he looked neat in his suit. His face was pleasant: He had large dark eyes and a beard, which I found kind of exotic. But I couldn't figure out how to relate to him, and I could tell my mom couldn't either: On the one hand, she was conversing with him like a contemporary; on the other hand, the way she touched his arm as if to guide him forward, and asked him where he planned to take me, seemed maternal.

"Well, you kids have fun," she said, kissing me on the cheek.

Barnett's car was a portly, middle-aged man's car—a Lincoln or maybe an Oldsmobile—and he took me to Café Sam, an upscale French restaurant that was, at the time, one of Pittsburgh's finest, with understated pale pink walls and tablecloths, and waiters who seemed offended by diners who did not wish to see the wine list. During lunch I felt like I was rehearsing for life in the post-college singles world as we discussed art, including a show at the Carnegie, a Pittsburgh museum.

When Barnett asked me what painters I liked, I wanted to sound sophisticated, but opted for honesty: "The impressionists, like Monet and Van Gogh."

"Of course," he said, not disrespectfully. "I like twentieth-century work like Dali and Kandinksy. But the impressionists are wonderful."

The whole time we chatted, I had the feeling of giving myself to him as a kind of gift, the sense—which was to recur in relationships for years to come—that in my youth, freshness, and vitality, with my sunny personality and pretty smile—I could make the difference in his life. It was a heady and pleasant feeling. Although I was far too young and lacking in confidence about my relationship skills to imagine much of a future, I believe that, having just seen *Last Tango in Paris* for the first time, I engaged in a few lurid fantasies about his strapping frame and my petite one intertwined.

Midway through the meal—skirt steak with lyonnaise potatoes for him and cold poached salmon for me—he made a confession about his ex-wife.

"She used to beat me," he said.

I tried not to react.

"Beat you?" I stammered.

"Yes," he sighed, clearing his throat, his rosebud mouth pursed beneath the neatly trimmed mustache and beard. Glancing at me, he continued.

"It's difficult to explain," he said. "It's not the kind of thing I would ever have thought would happen to me. You see, I come from the kind of family in which people are respectful of one another, where we solve problems verbally . . ."

"Of course," I said. I was stunned, and tried to imagine how this was possible.

". . . and, she had anger issues, and lots of problems. And I, well, I loved her. When you care about someone in that situation you just don't want to see it for what it is."

"I'm so sorry," I said. Even at my tender age, I had some intimation of the vicissitudes and even vileness some people endure in the name of love, and I felt sorry for Barnett, but this was too much. I carried on with the date, trying to imagine how a sophisticated woman like the Dazz would handle the situation.

"Well, I guess we've all been there, some way or another," I sighed. "Wasn't it Shakespeare who wrote, "Love Makes Fools of Us All?"

"In *A Midsummer Night's Dream*," said Barnett with a grateful smile.

He stared at me across the table with a gaze so open I felt uncomfortable. I looked down and rearranged my silverware, then opted to resume my pose as the young singleton.

"So what do you like to do on the weekends?" I asked. "What's the scene like around here?"

Barnett looked stung. I don't remember what he replied, but in retrospect I think he was a tad disappointed not to find a level of sensitivity and understanding from me that he'd hoped for. I did like him, and I felt sorry for him, but I was also trying to suppress giggles and looking forward to reporting his confession to the Dazz.

After lunch, Barnett drove me home, and at my mother's door he kissed me on the cheek. He did not ask me out again then and there, but within a couple days the word came via Mona that he had requested another date.

When I told the Dazz about Barnett's confession, we had a laugh. Within a couple of days, though, she was trying to convince me to go out with him again, because my mother is of the belief that everyone in pants should be given another chance.

As much as I love and admire her, I have learned through much trial and error to stop letting my mother fix me up. And while I still have my save-the-world tendencies, the empowerment I felt in not going out with Barnett again helped me realize that I don't have to be a gift for every awkward, lonely male.

Perfect Son-in-Law

Hemmy So

On my twenty-sixth birthday, my mother panicked.

Usually it's an age to celebrate, unless you're the traditional mother of a single Korean American woman.

My single life pained my mother, who suffered each time she heard about someone's amazing son-in-law buying a $2 million Manhattan apartment, a friend's Harvard-educated son-in-law making partner at a prestigious law firm, a church member's son-in-law humbly offering a Mercedes Benz as a meager thank-you-for-being-my-mother-in-law gift.

And their wives hadn't even reached twenty-six yet.

So when she found her Perfect Son-in-Law that autumn before my annual visit home for Christmas, the panic melted into bliss. Supposedly, he had everything she wanted: Korean blood, money, and what she called, loosely translated, "a malleable mind." (The last characteristic often helps regulate the second, she told me.)

"You can tell him what to do and he won't be fussy," she told me. "That's so important. You don't know yet, but that's so, so important."

My father is the one who discovered Dong Joon. He'd reconnected with an old buddy of his from South Korea, Dong Joon's father. To prepare his only son to inherit the family manufacturing company and fortune, Dong Joon's father sent him to the University of Houston to receive a Western education.

My mother kept his discovery a secret until I called to remind her about my flight home for the holidays.

"Hemmy-ya, I need you to do a favor. A Korean boy just moved here and he needs somebody to show him around," she said innocently. "He's so lonely!"

"Does he speak English?" I asked.

"Very little," she replied dismissively. "But you don't need to speak English to show him the neighborhood."

"I don't want to date him, Mom. He doesn't speak English. I can't even talk to this guy!"

My rudimentary command of the Korean language could get me through a night at the Korean restaurant, but I'd have to resort to pantomime and simple pencil drawings to discuss issues that can arise in relationships: politics, religion, children, life philosophy. How do you discuss healthcare using hand signs? How do you express your need for more emotional support through Pictionary?

My mom shot back a one-line response: "Love knows no language."

Right. I almost always end up giving into my mother. I have wondered if it's culturally stimulated guilt (while Americans say "I didn't ask to be born," Asians say "I owe my parents for being born"). Most times, I simply don't have the energy to argue.

On a gusty Christmas Eve, Perfect Son-in-Law showed up at our doorstep. He stood just a few inches taller than my mother, with short black hair gelled off to the side and noticeable wrinkles hugging the corners of his dotty eyes and thin mouth. His skin looked slightly leathery. He was shaped like a potato.

But more than anything, I immediately noticed the glaring signs of what many Asian Americans unapologetically call "F.O.B.," which stands for "fresh off the boat." Dong Joon wore classic Korean F.O.B. knock-off Burberry apparel: a beige button-down shirt accentuated with a not-quite-right tartan with skinny plaids, a red that's just a little too orange. His dirty white sneakers bore the trademark of a fashionable brand in Korea that never made it to America. I was not impressed.

After a perfunctory conversation with my parents, Perfect Son-in-Law drove me in his black Toyota Solara to Galveston Island, a touristy beach community near my parents' home in Houston.

Like many foreigners, he understood bits of English. So I spoke in "Kanglish," mixing English words with Korean ones.

"I live in New York. I'm a lawyer there," I said in Korean.

"Yes, your mother told me," Dong Joon said in Korean. "She is very proud of you."

"Mmm hmmm. I actually want to be a. . . ." I paused. What was the word for *journalist* in Korean?

"Journalist?" I said in English.

Blank look from Dong Joon. A loud hum from the engine.

I acted out a scene in which I opened a newspaper. I opened my arms wide and moved my head from side to side. I pointed to my imaginary broadsheet and started fake-typing.

"Yes, yes! Journalist," Perfect Son-in-Law said in Korean.

Not knowing whether he actually comprehended my charades since I couldn't confirm whether he had said "journalist" in Korean, I just nodded and smiled vigorously.

This would be a long date.

With most people at home celebrating the holidays, Galveston was barren. But determined to fulfill my mother's wish, I showed him the popular beach spots and shopping areas.

In keeping with this theatrical production known as "Act I: Showing a Newcomer the Touristy Spots," Perfect Son-in-Law whipped out his digital camera and took endless photos of me posing in front of empty restaurants, lonely plantation-style houses, and almost desolate beaches. When conversation lagged, he snapped a picture of me. It gave us something to do. It eased the discomfort of trying to get to know each other without the vocabulary to do it.

About an hour and a half had crept by, filled with short car rides from one venue to another, lots of snapshots and short Kanglish-cum-pantomime dialogues about simple subjects like beaches, Christmas, and family. Despite not wanting to be his future wife, I was curious about him. He had briefly mentioned an ex-girlfriend during our crippled conversations, and I wanted to know what happened with that relationship. Who dumped whom? Was the break-up the reason he agreed to meet me? Was it easier to have my mother arrange a marriage than to find a girl on his own? Or was he in the same predicament as me, suffering through a blind date to appease his family?

"Why did you tell my mom you'd go on a blind date with me?" I asked in Kanglish.

"I couldn't disrespect your mother and say no," he said. "You have to respect your parents. They want the best for us. I can find a girlfriend on my own, but sometimes parents know better."

The culture clash never echoed so loudly between two people. While I constantly challenged my parents with American ideas like chasing dreams, true love, and feminism, Perfect Son-in-Law still clutched the principles he grew up with.

The drive home took forty minutes and, as on the way to Galveston, his CDs kept us company. Once I arrived home, my mother and I felt relieved, but for different reasons. We didn't talk about the date.

Two days later I discovered, to my horror, that Perfect Son-in-Law liked me. My mother had spoken with Dong Joon on the phone and asked him: Did he see me as a future wife?

He told her he found me exceptionally charming, especially with my elementary-school Korean. My honesty captured his heart. I was very photogenic. I should have a second job as a tour guide. I explained American culture very well. And as a big, heart-felt thank you, he wanted to take me shopping.

This meant a second date with Dong Joon. My mother insisted on accompanying us because she wanted to be the one to pick out the Prada handbag he promised (in reality, my mother's trophy for "best matchmaking"). As this fifty-six-year-old Korean woman navigated the post-Christmas Neiman Marcus handbag department, Perfect Son-in-Law dutifully followed. I stood silently by the Christian Dior display cabinet, vacillating between disgust that this blind date charade had grown into a twisted relationship and equal disgust at my excitement at owning a $950 Prada bag. My mom picked it out: a bright orange tote with a nylon body, leather exterior pockets and leather straps.

I took the bag and ran back to New York.

No more Perfect Son-in-Law. Freedom to have crushes on non-Korean men who spoke English and avoided fake Burberry. Freedom to date imperfect men, including an overly metrosexual house DJ who once spent thirty-six hours playing video games. Freedom to make bad dating decisions.

Two months later, my mom called. Dong Joon would reenter my life.

"He's moving to New Jersey. He's going to go to school there. He'll be so close by! Show him around New York," she said.

"No, Mom, this is over. I am not showing him anything. I don't like him. He's not going to be my boyfriend."

Click.

Ring, ring, ring—for days.

"Fine. Have him call me."

Act II: Showing That Same Newcomer the Touristy Spots. In New York.

We had our painful, obligatory dinner in Manhattan at the original Palms restaurant. It was our first meal together. No Avril Lavigne to fill the dead air between us. Forced to converse, I asked him questions in Korean about his new school in New Jersey, whether he liked his new neighborhood.

I rushed through my meal, denied dessert (true sacrifice), and asked Dong Joon to drive me home. As we pulled up along East 25th Street, I said thanks and good-bye while ready to leap, if not tuck-and-roll, out of the car. He wanted a kiss.

The acrid taste of vomit crept into the back of my throat.

"I don't think so. See ya later."

"Can I at least come up for coffee?" he asked in Korean.

"No."

"But the dinner food made me so sleepy. I need caffeine. What if I'm driving across the bridge back to New Jersey and I fall asleep at the wheel? You'd be responsible for my death," he said with a straight face.

"I'm sorry, no," I said in English. I shrugged and hopped out of the car.

While I didn't see Perfect Son-in-Law in person for a few weeks, he made his presence known. He copied my name, title, and work address exactly as written on my business card and began sending me gifts addressed to "Hemmy W. So, Attorney-at-Law."

Another F.O.B. indicator, after fake Burberry, is sending Korean-style messages of affection: gifts of cultural relevance that are lost on Americans. A heart-shaped box filled with dozens of paper cranes colored with different highlighters went unappreciated. Letters written in English with excessively cute drawings in lieu of certain words were met with annoyance.

> *Dear Hemmy:*
> *I enjoyed our [insert cartoonish drawing of a plate of food]. I am so [insert smiling cartoon boy] that we can be such good friends. You make me [insert cartoon boy with mouth wide open and action signs showing laughter]."*

While I tried to ignore these outpourings of affection, my mother decided to visit. I forbade her from inviting Perfect Son-in-Law to my apartment. Our arguments over the matter exploded into ferocious screaming matches. But I never won because my mother never loses, especially when it came to the matter of her daughter's welfare. She didn't want me to endure hardships, struggle to make ends meet, or work eighty-hour weeks. She wanted me to live an easy life with kids and Prada handbags—even if that meant no romance.

"I do this because I love you," she would say. It's the same phrase she would use before whooping my ass as a child.

And not completely selflessly, she wanted Perfect Son-in-Law so she could have in-laws to whom she could relate. No language barriers, no cultural differences, no problems with the pungent smell of kimchi. In Korean culture, she told me, a family loses a daughter to her husband's family. And they wanted to give me away to someone they could trust.

Despite my efforts to avoid Dong Joon during my mother's visit, he finally showed up at my apartment one day, about thirty minutes after my mom and I had discussed shopping at Bloomingdale's. Apparently, my mom had snuck a phone call to him and invited him along. The last shopping trip together went so well, she thought, that a department store served as the perfect place for a reunion. She was wrong.

I lost it in the DKNY section.

"Stop stalking me, you freak! Just get away! I don't even like you," I yelled as I looking into his pudgy face.

"I am not a stalker," Perfect Son-in-Law shouted back in punctuated English.

People slowed their paces, they stared from behind the clothing racks, they stopped talking on their cell phones. I had created a scene but felt little regret at doing so.

I walked away, heading for the escalator, on my way to the subway entrance in the basement of Bloomingdale's. But not before I saw my mother's reaction.

She flushed with embarrassment, a rare emotion for her. Dong Joon felt victimized. A smidgen of guilt entered my heart, but the relief and victory felt too good to pay attention to that.

I never saw Perfect Son-in-Law again. My mother told me about two years later that he had gone back to Korea shortly after the Bloomingdale's incident, proposed to a cellist, and just had a baby boy. She didn't seem remorseful or nostalgic.

"Oh Hemmy-ya," my mom said over the phone, "there's a very nice, smart doctor in Galveston that we met through your father's friend. He's very smart. He speaks perfect English."

Well, at least she's making progress.

"This Person Is Perfect for You!"

Annie Downey

In the late nineties, after being dumped by the love of my life, I found myself, at the age of twenty-six, a full-time single mother of two kids under the age of seven, painting the interior of my house a different color until the wee hours of the morning in hopes of ridding the memories of my ex from my home.

That night—while my ex was partying it up with a bunch of hot, childless gals who were unfettered by diapers, school schedules, and runny noses—I was wearing my usual cut-off shorts, dipping my paint roller into a particularly gruesome color of bright orange, seeing myself as the biggest loser in the world, certain I would be alone for the rest of my life.

Having exhausted all my girlfriends with my perpetual whining over being dumped, I knew my mother (a dumpee like myself) would be the only person who would still take a call from me after midnight. She picked up on the first ring.

"I've decided to become a lesbian," I announced in a tone that sounded like I had been thinking about it for a while. Truth be told, I hadn't, though I had a lot of friends who were lesbians.

On the phone with my mother, I went on to bitch about how I hated the whole male race, and my mom responded with her usual PC-hippy-who-works-at-a-co-op way, "I know exactly what you mean," or "I couldn't agree more." After a good hour of venting and painting, we chimed our usual "hang in there," and I felt comforted enough to collapse in an exhausted heap on my bed.

A little before Christmas (the newly single mother's most vulnerable period for full-blown hysteria, throwing herself under a truck, and desperate dating measures), my mom called to tell me that she had found the perfect person for me to date. She had never cared about my dating life—*only* my dumpee life—so I asked suspiciously, "Really?"

"Really. Chris is a single parent just like you and, well, very attractive. And has the same creative flare as you—is really into natural parenting. I'm telling you—Chris is perfect!"

"Where did you meet Chris?" I asked.

"We work together," she answered.

"At the co-op?"

"That is where I work. So, yes."

"Is he some hippy-loser who works in the produce section?"

"No, this person happens to be a landscaper."

"*A landscaper*," I gasped. I instantly imagined six-pack abs, bulging pecks, and arms of steel dumping loads of dark organic soil onto raised beds. He definitely wore a bandana, crinkled his eyes in this endearing yet thoughtful way when he spoke, and had a small amount of rugged stubble on his chin. In my crazy-dumpee-pre-Christmas-desperation I went so far as envisioning him in his small Toyota vegetable oil–fueled pick-up truck packed full of organic brown rice, beeswax candles, and natural sunscreen picking up his little beautiful earthen child at the Waldorf School.

"Of course if you're not interested, I won't pursue the issue," my mother continued.

As I surfaced from my fantasy-daze, I questioned foggily, "What issue?"

"Of you two meeting when you come for Christma—"

"Meeting?"

"Yes—*meeting*. That's what two people do when they lay eyes on each other for the first time—*they meet*," my mother responded.

A vile vision interrupted my fools fantasy: Me, with my two–toned, shaggy, dried-out, dyed hair and haunted skeletal frame, meeting him for the first time, and then blurting out my whole horrible break up story, using words like "bastard" and "cock-sucker" to emphasize how much pain I was in. Because that is what I looked like and telling my horrible break-up story is all I did. I couldn't help myself. I told my horrible break-up story to cashiers at the grocery store, bank tellers, and even little unsus-pecting old ladies on their way to church—*anyone* who had not heard the story before.

"I don't think I am ready to meet anyone just yet," I told my mother, toying with the phone cord.

"Suit yourself," she said curtly, and hung up the phone with-out saying goodbye.

As the day went on I couldn't get the idea of the landscaper out of my head. I began to consider that maybe—just maybe—there really was a perfect guy out there for me and I was blowing my one chance to meet him. Unable to stand it anymore, I called her up and said, "Fine. I'll meet this landscaper of yours."

"Good. I think it would be good for you. Then you'll know whether or not you—you know—"

"I'm crazy? I'm demented? An ax-murderer?" I interrupted.

"Don't be silly," my mother said. "Listen, I have a friend over from work—"

"The landscaper?"

"No. Not the landscaper. I'll call you in the morning."

The next day my mother told me that she'd set up a time for me and the landscaper to meet (the day after Christmas). Suddenly, I had this new little thrill to help me weather the upcoming holiday. I started eating again. I made Christmas cookies. I dyed my hair back to dark brown and had the hairdresser cut it into a Cleopatra-looking bob. I bought new lingerie. I put little stick-ums up around the house reminding me not to talk about my break-up. I stopped painting the interior of my house. I started wearing pants. My friends started coming around again. They told me I looked "good," or rather, "more like myself," I was convinced I was now on the road to recovery. That I was about to meet my perfect match. I felt tremendous gratitude toward my mother—because of her I had a second chance at love! But the fact that I trusted my mother to set me up with anyone at all, let alone the new love of my life, should have been fair warning that I had officially lost *all* bearing on reality.

The day after Christmas was cold, so cold, that my eyes began to tear the moment I stepped out of the house. I ran to my car in my little sexy outfit, turned on the ignition, and honked and waved to my children who stood peering out the front door with my mother. They waved back, and I zoomed away with my heart fluttering like a schoolgirl's.

The landscaper and I were scheduled to meet at the co-op parking lot at 1:00 P.M. I was told to look for a beat-up yellow VW bus. As the car warmed up and I jetted along the back roads, I began to make my introduction out loud. "Hi, it is so nice to meet you. My mother told me so many nice things about you. Oh! It was so nice of you to bring me a blooming orchid! And this time of the year! You must have a real green thumb! Oh! Are those muscles real? Oh, my gosh! They are! Sure, I would love to go back to your cabin and snuggle up under bear skin while you play the guitar—no problem—my mother said she would take the kids for the night!"

When I got to the co-op parking lot there was no VW in sight. I let my car idle in a parking space and tried to still my heart by applying make-up and then wiping it off. A half hour or so later, a yellow VW bus rolled into the lot, and a woman with short hair hopped out of the driver's side. I sat up straighter. Fear wrapped itself around me. I was sure this woman was the landscaper's new girlfriend and had gotten wind of our little rendezvous and was about to give me a piece of her mind—or worse. It suddenly made sense why he was late . . . what's her name who was now bearing down on my car like a rabid animal had found out right before he was about to hop in the car and had killed him. I was so freaked out that I didn't have the good sense to lock the doors or screech out of the parking lot. Instead, I sat, watching the woman strut across the parking lot and motion for me to roll my window down. I rolled it down, the cold air hitting my dumb smile.

"Annie?" she asked. Her tone was pleasant enough.

"Yes?" I asked, dumbly smiling.

"I'm Chris."

"Yes?" I questioned again, still trying to smile.

"Your mom said we should meet."

I looked at her Cartharts, her thick wool sweater, and her muck boots.

"Are you a landscaper?" I asked, hoping beyond hope that there was some awful mix-up and another Chris (who wasn't dead and lying in a pool of blood or a woman with a blond pixie cut) in a yellow VW bus was on his way.

"Mmmm," she nodded.

I gripped the steering wheel and tried to figure out why my mother would do this to me. Why, why, why? Then, remembering the night I announced I had decided to be a lesbian, combined with my mother's choice of words—"this person is perfect for you"—it suddenly was all too clear. My mother, in her PC, co-op fashion, had been trying to embrace what she thought was my new found lifestyle.

"Oh holy mother of god," I mumbled.

"What was that?" Chris asked, thinking I had said something to her, and afraid of hurting her feelings, I turned off the engine of my car, swung my door open, and shakily removed myself from my vehicle.

"I was just starting to say—my mother has told me so much about you," I said.

"I hope it's been all good things," she said, her face pinched.

"More than good," I added, trying to cover my misery. "As far as she's concerned, you're perfect."

The co-op café is, well, *very small*, and the only seating available was a rickety and crumb-ridden table near the restroom. It was also the place where my mother worked. People knew me. They also knew Chris. I would have to be really careful not to create a situation in which this woman would start screaming and cursing or—worse—*crying*.

I decided to keep playing dumb. After we unpeeled the many layers of winter clothing, ordered a pot of green tea (I hate green tea), and were safely seated near the lovely odor of au-de-toilette, Chris proceeded to lean her chair back, steaming cup in hand, and give me a shy smile. She told me about her childhood. How she never "fit" and then went on to tell me about her failed marriage. As she talked she fiddled with her ear and then gave a sigh.

It was completely endearing and heartbreaking. I felt terrible. I couldn't keep up this façade. I knew I should confess about the misunderstanding. But as much as I tried to get the words out, I couldn't because I imagined all the other hippies who worked there, scratching their dread-locked heads, and saying to my mother: "But I thought you said your daughter was a lesbian?" She'd look like an idiot.

And there was this innocent woman to think of. It was obvious by her earnest expression she was interested in me. "It's been a long time since I did this dating thing," she said as she nervously put her tea down on the table. "Do you go on a lot of dates? Sorry I asked that. That is none of my business. I guess I meant to ask, are you looking for a long-term relationship?" She twiddled, then sighed.

My heart bled for her.

She was so like me when I was instantly head-over-heels for someone. I looked back upon all the boys and men who had not been attracted to me. No matter how nice they'd been about it—it had inevitably ended with me in tears and storming out.

I decided to change the subject to our children.

"Oh, my son is real mellow," Chris said. "I don't know where he gets it, because I'm kind of hyper." She twiddled and sighed again. "We live in a cabin way out, and it is just me and him most of the time—it gets a little isolating. It's hard to meet people."

I nodded my head rapidly. Like I knew exactly what it was like to live in a cabin in the boonies. Chris sat staring at me from across the table. Her kind blue eyes filled with need, and she suddenly looked so lonely. *Maybe I could become a lesbian*, I thought. I imagined myself marrying Chris and living with her in the cabin—boiling water on the wood stove for a bath and hanging our kids' clothes out on the line. The Holly Hobby clothes that

I would get to wear. Chris wasn't unattractive. As I looked at her masculine face, her full lips, and the light hairs on her wiry arms, I thought—maybe if I just gave it a try. . . .

I quickly looked down at my teacup, concentrating on a small bit of honey oozing down the side. "So, do you want to catch a movie or something?" I asked her. "My mother has my kids tonight."

The store went quiet. It was as if every member of the co-op were waiting for her answer. I could hear the clock tick.

Finally, Chris swallowed and said gently, "I don't want to hurt your feelings, but you're really not my type—you know—physically. I don't really go for skinny girls. I know there's a lot of women who do—I'm just not one of them." Her face scrunched a little with this obvious distaste over my bony frame.

I looked at her with an incredulous expression.

"Sorry," she said.

Finally I spoke, "I've actually gained weight. You should have seen how skinny I was *before*—right after my ex *dumped me*. . . ."

And I went on and on and on. . About how I threw out every piece of jewelry he'd ever given me. How I cut up every photo with him and me in it (that was actually a lie—I gave them back to him so he would remember how wonderful it was to be with me . . . it didn't work). About how I sprinkled salt in every corner, lit sage, stuck pins in a little doll, mediated, took antidepressants . . . but only for a week until my toe turned numb. And about how I just couldn't seem move on.

"Do you think I'm nuts to still love a guy that dumped me and left me to raise a one year old by myself?" I asked her.

"Ummm . . . no," she said unconvincingly.

"Why can't I just get over him? *Why*?" I asked, now hysterical. "Do you know what is really funny? He liked skinny girls—

I was too fat when we were together. But what did he expect—
I just had a baby!"

Chris eventually gathered her things, mumbled something
about picking up her son and fled.

When I dragged my insanely-skinny-dumpee-butt back
home, my mother greeted me at the door with a worried look.

"I was just joking about being a lesbian!" I screamed. "And
even if I hadn't been joking, it turns out even women aren't into
me!" and promptly burst into tears.

"Oh, honey, I'm sorry!" she said, throwing her arms around
me. "Women, men, they're all the same! They're all assholes!"

"Tell me about it," I said, wiping my eyes.

"Come on, I made my famous apple crisp and I took the kids
to the video store and we got a bunch of movies."

And as we ate our crisp and all of us watched some cartoon
manifestation of a love story—my mother turned to me and
said, "This is nice. Who needs men when you can have this
instead."

"Or women," I said, and smiled.

Dentists & Dragons

Aury Wallington

"I've written a screenplay," Dr. Steve told my mom. He adjusted the light over her chair, then examined his progress on her back teeth with a tiny tilted mirror. "It's a high-concept fantasy blockbuster about a dentist who treats dragons. I call it Fire, Fang, and Floss. *Catchy, right?"*

My mom couldn't answer, since he had his fingers in her mouth, along with considerable amounts of blood and bits of tooth enamel. So she just lifted her eyebrows and gave him an encouraging gurgle.

"I see Jude Law as the dentist," he continued, gouging at her jaw with a pair of Civil War–era serrated clippers. "It's a. . . ."

"I thought you were just having your teeth cleaned," I interrupted, shifting the phone to my other ear, "and—he used serrated clippers? *Really?*"

She thought about this for a second. "Well, it might have been a bone saw."

My mother's always had a near-pathological fear of dentists and the pain that they can inflict. She panics at even the most routine checkup, and her terror was worsened by the fact that her regular dentist, Dr. Manfredi, whom she had been seeing for the past five years, had recently retired.

She'd had an appointment that morning with the guy who took over Dr. Manfredi's practice, and since I knew how worried she'd been about seeing someone new, I called to check in.

"At least it's over and done with now," I said, wandering into the bathroom and peering at my own teeth in the mirror. "You won't have to go through that again for another six months."

"Actually, I found out I need to have two bridges replaced," she said. "I have another appointment in three weeks."

"Oh, no!"

"I'm sure it'll be fine," she said.

She was?! I frowned into the phone, suspicious.

"I mean, I got so absorbed in hearing about his screenplay that I barely even noticed him roto-tilling my gums. And he seemed really excited when I told him my daughter lives in Hollywood. . . ."

Oh god. "You didn't tell him to send it to me, did you?"

"I thought you'd be interested," she said, in a voice way too innocent to be convincing. "It's a cross between *Lord of the Rings* and *Steel Magnolias*. Action *and* heart. Dr. Steve and I both think it's a slam dunk."

I shut my eyes for a second, taking a deep calming yoga breath. "I can't even get anyone to look at my own stuff," I told her. "How am I supposed to help him?"

"Just read it. Give him some notes. Some constructive criticism."

"Here's a note: Don't write movies about dragon dentists."

"I'm scheduled for extensive bridgework!" she shrilled suddenly. "If your reading his script is what it takes to make that sadist give me enough Novocain that I don't faint dead away when he hatchets through my molars, then you can damn well read his script!"

She isn't usually like this, I swear. Only when it comes to dentists.

"Fine," I said, "I'll read it. Have him give you a hard copy to send to me—"

"Oh, he can just give it to you himself," she said, "when you go out on your date next week. Dr. Steve is flying out to California for some convention, so I said you'd have dinner with him."

"Are you kidding?"

"He's not unattractive. And when I told him you were single, he was very interested."

Pimped out for painkillers. I felt like Janis Joplin's daughter or something.

I'd moved to Los Angeles from New York a year earlier to take a job writing for a new TV show, leaving behind a boyfriend, an apartment, and a full and happy life. I didn't mind the sacrifice, since I was planning to set the world on fire with my writing.

Instead, ratings on the show fizzled, I was having zero luck selling my own screenplay, and while I had found a great new apartment, I was coming up dry in the boyfriend department. I hadn't had a date in nearly eleven months. And with the hangover from my thirtieth birthday party officially worn off, I knew I had to get back into the game before age-related injuries kept me from playing. So when Dr. Steve called to make plans for our date, I tried to make the best of it.

"Do you want to come to the convention with me?" he asked. His voice was high and nasal, like he was imitating the sound of his drill while he talked. "It's going to be a blast."

Ooh, Saturday night at a dental convention—what more could a girl ask for? "Uh . . ." I said, shrugging even though we were on the phone, "sure, I guess."

"You don't mind getting dressed up, do you?"

"I love getting dressed up." Maybe it would be a good date after all.

After I hung up, I looked up Dr. Steve's picture on my mom's insurance provider's Web site. My mom was right. He *wasn't* unattractive. It was a little hard to make out his exact features since he was wearing one of those oral-surgery headlamps that reflected into the camera, but dark curly hair, no visible scars, and a mouthful of perfect teeth gave a general impression of cute.

Plus, I figured, he *was* a doctor, sort of. *And* a screenwriter. And he was taking me somewhere fancy. Maybe it wouldn't be so bad. Maybe we would even fall in love and look back on this date as the first step in our new lives together. The more I thought about it, the more positive I felt, and by the day of our actual date, I had worked myself up into a state of happy anticipation.

I put on my favorite dress, a knee-length plum silk shift with spaghetti straps, and my Miu Miu kitten-heeled slingbacks. I spent a long time on my makeup and was just finishing blow-drying my hair perfectly straight when the doorbell rang.

I took a deep breath and opened the door.

An elf was standing on my front porch.

Or, more accurately, a grown man dressed as an elf. And not a hot, Orlando Bloom–type elf, either, but the kind who repairs all the shoes while the cobbler's asleep. The curly hair and huge shining teeth convinced me he was the same guy from his Web picture, but he had traded in the headlamp for a green tunic, a little peaked hat, and curly-toed boots.

I thought he was going to offer to cover something in fudge for me. Instead, he put a script in my hand.

"Hi, Aury, I'm Dr. Steve! Thanks so much for reading this. I really appreciate it."

I was too flabbergasted to understand what was going on. Was the elf costume a gimmick to entice me to read the script? He was also holding a garment bag. I really hoped his tux was in it, but he gave it to me too. "Here you go."

"What's this?"

"Your costume."

What?

"You said you wanted to dress up, right?"

I *did* say that.

"So . . . we're going to a costume party?" I asked. Even though I was annoyed I was still confused.

"No, we're going to the convention."

"But why are we wearing costumes to a dental convention?"

"*Dental* convention?" Now Dr. Steve looked confused. "What are you talking about? We're going to the SoCal GenCon Gamers' Convention. We're going to play in a live-action Dungeons and Dragons game."

Oh. My. God.

Turned out I didn't need to read the screenplay after all—Dr. Steve recited it to me, line by excruciating line, on the two-hour drive to the convention center in Anaheim.

I squirmed in the passenger seat, trying to keep the ridiculously short and tight sequined skirt from riding up. My whole outfit was ridiculous, from the peacock feathers adorning the conical Maid Marion hat to the silk ribbons on the sandals, which Dr. Steve had insisted I tie gladiator-style up my calves. And the dress itself, a ghastly spangled sausage-casing which could only be a result of my mother lying to him about how thin I was—or, clearly, *wasn't.*

By the time we finally reached the convention center parking lot, Dr. Steve was regaling me with the final climactic battle of his script, doing different voices to act out the dashing young dentist, Shane Trueheart, and the evil dragon-killer, Devlin Maldoro. I had given up on trying to keep my dress covering my knees and was staring catatonically out the side window, desperately praying that the Gamers' Convention would have an open bar.

A few moments later we stood at the registration desk outside the entrance to the Dungeon. "Okay, what's your name?" Dr. Steve asked me.

I looked down at him, confused by the question but grateful that at least the stacked heels on his boots brought his eyes up above cleavage-level. ". . . Aury," I answered.

"No—not your name, your *elfin* name," he said. "I'm Garnok, Dental Warrior!"

"Greetings, Garnok!" said the pimply guy who was signing us in. He was dressed in a costume that looked like Yoda but probably wasn't supposed to. "I see you've brought us a virgin!"

"That's what they call new gamers," Dr. Steve told me, giggling.

I tried not to let them see me roll my eyes.

"So—name?"

"Uh . . . 'Snap,'" I said, thinking of the elf from the Rice Krispies box.

"Good. Now you have to roll to determine your character traits." Dr. Steve handed me a pair of ten-sided dice. "You're trying to get the highest number possible. Twenty is the best. First, roll for strength."

I rolled. "Seventeen."

"That's great! Roll again."

I did, and his face dropped. "Oh. An eight in charisma."

"What does that mean?" I asked, giving the bottom of my naughty nymph costume another half-hearted tug to try to get it to cover more of my legs.

"Um, you're not exactly going to be winning any beauty contests." Steve let out a little snort, and the jingle-bells he had sewn around the collar of his tunic tinkled merrily.

Yoda cackled too. "Are you kidding? With an eight charisma, you could scare the monsters away with your face."

I gave him a you're-one-to-talk look, then turned back to Dr. Steve, as a couple guys in doofy-looking Viking hats crowded up to the registration desk behind us.

"Is that it?" I asked him, figuring the sooner we started playing, the sooner we could stop.

"Almost. We just need to roll for THACO, get your hit points and saving throws, and buy you some armor, then we'll be all set."

Jesus Christ. "Listen, Dr. Steve—"

"Garnok!"

Sigh. "Listen, Garnok, I think I might just wait for you in the car . . . "

"No!" he said, grabbing my arm and giving me a pleading look. "Come on, give it a try. It's really fun. I promise."

"Fine," I said, if only to spare my mom any drill-style retribution. "I'll play."

"Whoo!" Yoda cheered. "The quest is afoot!"

The point of the game, Dr. Steve explained, was to decipher symbols on a map Yoda had given us and collect magical items as we made our way to the final chamber, where we would free a princess and claim a treasure.

Interesting enough in theory, but in practice felt like a cross between dinner at Medieval Times and an excruciatingly slow-paced horror flick.

The convention center had been turned into a catacomb. Multicolored mist from smoke machines swirled around our feet and eerie thumps and snarls were piped in over the PA system. Dozens of shrouded clerics and wizards raced through the passageways, shouting things like "By Hornung's Faerie Fire, I command thee: Open!" and "Scurrilous knave, you'll feel the lick of my shillelagh yet!"

In each new room we entered, we had to fight and defeat actors dressed like rejects from a Gwar video, who brandished big reaper-style scythes which they vowed to disembowel us with. Only, instead of us doing any real fighting, which might at least have been exciting, everyone stopped and pulled out their dice.

"I strike you with my horseman's mace!" Dr. Steve declared, and rolled. Then we waited in silence while the Dungeon Master, a twelve-year-old boy who followed us from room to room, consulted his charts.

"You inflict three points of damage."

Then it was Gwar's turn to roll. "I shoot you in the chest with my crossbow."

The Dungeon Master flipped through his charts. "Miss!"

"Victory is mine!" Dr. Steve shouted, doing a double-fist-pump into the air, while I doubled my efforts to find a bar.

Then we walked into the next room and did the exact same thing all over again.

And again; and again; and again. For *five hours.*

By the time we'd rescued the princess and finished the game, I was so wiped out that I was seriously considering drinking the nail polish I had in my purse because at least it was *something* alcoholic.

On the way back home I slumped in my seat as Dr. Steve drove, barely able to respond to his enthusiastic recap of the game we'd just played with more than an occasional grunt or nod. When we finally got to my apartment, he pulled the car up to the curb and cut the engine.

"So. Can I come inside for a while?"

Was he joking? "I don't think so. I'm pretty tired."

He shifted closer to me on the seat. I shifted away.

"I'll, um, have the costume dry-cleaned and send it to my mom to give back to you," I said.

"Or you could take it off right now!" He leaned his body forward like he was going to kiss me. I scooted back even farther until I was pressed against the passenger door.

"That's okay."

"Come on," he insisted, walking his fingers up my knee. "I've got one more dragon for you to tame."

I looked at him, from his pit-stained tunic to his pom-pom-fringed cape to his sparkly white chompers, and made a decision.

"Tell you what," I said. "You can roll for it."

Dr. Steve grinned and pulled out his dice one last time. He rolled them on the dashboard.

"Nineteen!" he crowed, leaning in again, closing his eyes as he puckered up.

I took a deep breath. It was after midnight; eight hours ago, I'd had started the evening thinking maybe things would work out between me and Dr. Steve. But since then, I had given up any hope or desire for that to happen. I'd also developed a deep and lasting hatred of the convention center and everyone in it, learned how to say "get your hand off my ass" in Druid, lost every shred of personal dignity I possessed, and killed a total of sixteen Orcs with a throwing hammer and bag of poison darts.

The date had been the worst of my life. And I knew if I didn't kiss him now, I would have to add "disappointed my mother" to the list.

I reached for the handle of the car door. "Miss!"

Dr. Steve's eyes flew open in shock.

"Sorry, Garnok," I said, leaping out of the car. "Guess this time, victory is *mine*."

As I headed up the walkway to my apartment Dr. Steve started up the car, the tires squealing angrily as he drove away.

So my mom wouldn't get her Novocain. Oh well.

There are worse things than pain.

Mother Knows,
Even When She Doesn't

Melissa Pheterson

I arrived in Manhattan five years ago, ready to fall in love. But after blind dating, speed dating, office dating, and many misbegotten set-ups from well-meaning acquaintances, I concluded that romance was not to be found anywhere on the grid—or even down in the Village.

My mother, Carol, ensconced in her upstate hamlet 330 miles away, began patrolling my J-date account to find suitable men. She remained chirpily optimistic, drawing comfort from the statistics she found on frequent Web crawls. "There are millions of single men in New York," she said. "I read it on Wikipedia." To give me the edge in an online catalog teeming with similar goods, Mom would "update" my profile by adding or deleting words like "the" or "and," catapulting me to the top of the list with a flashing "NEW" sign. To thank her for this service, I let her read every e-mail in my J-date dossier.

Giggling like schoolgirls, we copied and pasted chats and profiles to share online, tag-teaming from our respective command centers: mine a laptop perched on a cluttered IKEA desk; hers a wide-screen Dell built into a wall unit in her den.

But I soon grew tired of lackluster dates, and men that hid behind their monitors. So I begged Mom to do some off-line networking, and scout for dates in the Rochester suburbs. My parents had lived there for two years, and had only begun to untangle the threads that linked everyone in at least three ways. Women her age had sons my age, and many still lived close to home, suggesting a boy-next-door mentality I sorely missed. I could hop a flight for a weekend date; I'd once taken the subway to Brooklyn, hadn't I?

One autumn evening, Mom attended a meeting of the Rochester branch of the Jewish Women's International social action group. The chapter president, Roberta, was hosting the meeting at her Wedgwood-blue home with white shutters. My mother scanned the family photos that crowded the walls, coffee tables, counters, and mantels. Nearly all featured a guy that looked my age, with a dimpled chin, coffee-brown eyes and a head of lustrous chestnut curls. My mom waylaid Roberta and asked, in the same breath: "Is that your son? Is he single?"

"Yes to both," Roberta said. "Josh is at Harvard Law School. But this summer, he'll be working in Manhattan."

That did it: My mother's radar was going nuts. (Also, I had so emphatically pleaded, "No baldies!" that she must have been smitten by the hair, before the brain it covered.)

As the summer approached, my mother called Roberta to rally for a date.

"He's not that tall," Roberta hedged. Unfazed, my mother replied: "She doesn't need tall. She needs *smart*!" Roberta gave Josh my number, and we arranged to meet for a drink at Merchants New York, near Bloomingdales.

He was cute; my mother (and the pictures) hadn't lied. At a respectable five-foot-seven, he had three inches on me. And he was dressed in a suit, as required by his summer-associate position at a large firm. I wore jeans and an azure blouse, as casual as he was corporate.

We greeted each other tentatively, shook hands and grabbed a table overlooking First Avenue. I primed myself for the usual first-date drivel: work, food, movies. Smiling and tossing my hair, I leaned in. "How do you like New York?"

"I like it," he said, brusquely. "Would you care for a drink?"

He seemed bored with small talk, impatient with niceties. I wondered if I qualified as date material for Harvard men. He didn't offer to buy me dinner, but we did check out the appetizer menu. I watched as he scanned both sides with freaky speed-reading ability. "I hate cheese," he said defiantly, as if daring me to stick up for it. "It has an offensive texture. But I like scallops wrapped in bacon." *Yuck*, I thought.

He ordered a beer; I chose the house white wine.

"The house white?" he said, teasingly. "Didn't you take Wines at Cornell?" Our mothers had informed us that we had graduated from the same school, same year.

"No," I said, a little miffed. "I had a double major. No time for electives."

"Ah," he said. "So you were a dork." His jaw dropped into a smile, and he poked out his tongue. "I only used the library to check e-mail. I never have to study."

"Not even at Harvard?"

He shrugged. "It's not that hard, I barely go to class. I compose my papers in my head. Sometimes while I'm at the casino."

As a textbook overachiever, I bristled at this. Our drinks arrived, none too soon, and I gulped down a mouthful. "It's a fine vintage," I said, defensively. It could have been cat piss, for all I knew.

As I drank, my irritation receded into wry amusement. At least he wasn't falsely modest. He asked me, occasionally, about my grad school work and future aspirations. But he seemed to relish holding court. When the bill came, he signed his name with two quick strokes.

"Thanks for the drink," I said.

"How about a walk?" he asked, standing up and stuffing his hands in his pockets, gesturing with his head. "After you. . . ."

We cut east toward the river, and I tried to relax and enjoy the twilight. Still locked in overdrive, Josh was musing on the "boot camp" experience of summer law associates. I privately disagreed. Even my halfhearted gym workouts, I thought, were more rigorous than yammering legalese from a plush desk chair and getting taken to Nobu for lunch. I studied the ground to make sure my heels wouldn't catch in anything. Two feet away, a rat darted under the walkway railing. I jumped.

Josh halted his monologue. "Are you okay?" he said.

"There's a rat nearby," I said, weakly.

He chuckled. "You girls are scared of everything. I'm only teasing!" he protested, baring that sponge-pink tongue. "Come on, I'll take you home."

"Okay," I said, shrugging. In the crush of his decisiveness, I was powerless to argue. He walked me back to my apartment, wrapping up the loose ends of his life story.

"Oh look, there's my doorman," I murmured. "I haven't spoken with him in forever." Awkward moments weren't my thing, and I had no idea how Josh planned to say good night. He seemed awfully fond of extending his tongue.

"Well, it was nice to meet you," he said, pulling me into a perfunctory hug. "I had a good time." Then he turned and strode down the block.

Back in my apartment, I called my mother to throw a damp cloth on her enthusiasm. "He bragged nonstop and didn't offer to buy me dinner," I sniffed, giving voice to my inner pessimist. Moreover, I was growing increasingly certain that cheese was my absolute favorite food, and I couldn't possibly commit to a man who would not gaze adoringly into my eyes over a bubbling cauldron of Swiss fondue.

The next morning I received an e-mail from Josh stating that he'd had a good time, but didn't see a romantic connection: essentially, good bye and good luck. I forwarded the e-mail to my girlfriend. "Classic pre-emptive move," she said over prosecco that night. "He rejected you before you could reject him." Then she cocked her head. "You *were* going to reject him, right?"

I shrugged.

In summer 2006, I moved home to Rochester. Before she helped me unpack, my mother changed the zip code settings on J-date to scout for local prospects. Browsing profiles one night, she saw the curly-haired lawyer who had recently migrated north from Manhattan.

My mom knocked on the bathroom door and shouted over the running shower, "Guess who's back in town? Josh Pheterson!"

"Great," I said, scrubbing my leg furiously.

"Call him," she pleaded. "Maybe you'll hit it off this time."

"But he rejected me," I whined.

An hour later, I relented. I was just bored enough to figure, *what the hell*, and e-mail his mother.

One week later, he wrote at 3:00 A.M. saying it was nice to hear from me and giving me his number. I called him the next day after lunch, probably before he arose, and he called my cell an hour later. I was taking a walk through the woods behind my parents' house.

"Hey, Josh," I said, nervous despite myself. "How's it going?" I kicked at a twig and fished for something to say. *How've you been for the past thousand days?*

"Good, how 'bout you?" he parried back, easily. My fuzzy recollections quickly sharpened into focus.

We discovered that we had both moved to Rochester after becoming disenchanted with the city. I joked to him that we could team up here, a region that suffered from major "brain drain," to find suitable romantic prospects—escorting each other to happy hours and playing "wingman." He readily agreed. "We should break into the med student circle," he declared.

We decided on dinner the next night, at an Asian place called Mamasan's Noodle Caboodle. "I pick up food there every day," he explained.

That day I slipped on a lacy pink camisole and denim miniskirt, aiming to look as sexy as possible. I would make him good and sorry that he didn't like me.

"Whoever he is," my father said, "he's a lucky guy."

"He didn't feel a romantic connection," I demurred.

"Well, he will now," said Mom.

I arrived a little before him, lingered in the entryway, and saw him pull up in a red Honda. He strode in past the wire-sculpture flowers that were oxidizing on the patio. He looked a bit heavier, and more casually dressed this time in a salmon-colored Polo shirt that matched my camisole. But still—those glorious curls!

"Hello, Counselor!" the Asian woman at the register chirped. "Usual tonight?"

I cleared my throat. "Hey, Josh," I said, with knee bent and hand on hip. Maybe he would at least admit to himself that, objectively, I wasn't bad-looking, and set me up with one of his high-school friends.

"How've you been?" he said, all business, as if he'd just seen me the week before. So much for an emotional reunion.

We sat outside, breathing in the exhaust fumes of the SUVs barreling down the road and sipping chilled wine.

"So what have you been up to the past three years?" he asked.

"Eh," I said. "Bad relationship, boring job, pointless grad program."

"Oh, yeah?" he said, grinning. "You should hear my dating and work horror stories."

"Oh, do tell," I said. I knew that "the rules" advised girls to accentuate the positive on dates, keep things sparkly and upbeat. But, hey, this wasn't a date.

And so we bonded over our gripes, rehashing our tragicomic urban adventures. Between bites of Cashew Chicken, he made me laugh—and very nearly cry. Had he been so witty, so sweet, three years back? I felt a spark of intrigue. Could I let myself like him?

Before we opened our fortune cookies, he asked me whether we could go out on an official date.

"I'd love to," I said, and meant it. Then I paused. "Just don't let me get an e-mail from you retracting the offer," I said, wagging my finger. "Do you even remember anything about our first date?"

"Sure," he said. "You wore blue. And you were stand-offish."

"Well, you were arrogant," I teased.

"I'm very arrogant," he agreed.

We drove over to the strip-mall Starbucks for coffee, then took a walk in the cul-de-sac behind it. Five minutes in, he took my cup of Chai from my hand, set it on someone's lawn, and kissed me.

When I got home, I heard my mother on the phone from her bedroom. "Harvard Law School," she was whispering. "The father's an attorney."

I cleared my throat.

"Oh, bye!" she blurted, snapping her phone shut. "So how was it?" My dad bounded up the stairs to hear.

I sunk into the chair. "I think he likes me," I whispered, defeated. I hate when parents turn out to be right.

When he called the next day, I impulsively invited him to my house for a barbecue. Because one guest was vegetarian, we served a menu of Boca burgers with cheese and gazpacho shooters. Josh arrived first, departed last, laughed at everything I said, and touched nothing on his plate.

"He likes you," Mom said. "He clearly didn't come for the food."

We began to date, and a few weeks later, moved in together—a lickety-split courtship that rendered even our mothers speechless. When we got engaged, we met with the Rabbi and answered her query into how we met. "Our moms set us up," I said.

"Twice," Josh added.

"The timing wasn't right at first," I said.

"She was a cold fish," Josh explained.

For five years, I'd begged and sometimes paid matchmakers, rabbis, professors, cousins, friends, and coworkers to find me a man. But I came away with one lesson: If you want something done right, ask your mother.

About *the* Contributors

KAREN ALEXANDER is a writer living in Berkeley, California.

⊰⧆⊱

TARA BAHRAMPOUR is a staff writer at the *Washington Post* and the author of the memoir *To See and See Again: A Life in Iran and America* (Farrar, Straus & Giroux), which traces her family's migrations between Iran and the United States and her own journey back to Iran as an adult. She has written for the *New Yorker*, the *New York Times*, the *American Scholar*, and other publications. She lives in Washington, D.C.

⊰⧆⊱

LOIS BARTH is a life coach (specializing in relationship and work/life balance), workshop leader, and writer. She is the life coach for *Fitness* magazine's, Fitness Makeover, She wrote and performed her one-woman show, "1001 Dates from Hell. . . . And the Woman Who Lived Through Them." She has received three *Poets and Writers* grants, has been published in the *New York Times*, and was featured on *Good Day New York*. Having gone from ludicrous no-night stands to a luscious life partnership, she is a gratefully retired serial dater. She can be reached at *www.1Dreamatatime.com*.

SARA BARRON is the author of the essay collection *People Are Unappealing* (Three Rivers Press). She has published humor and nonfiction in the anthology *Mortified: The Big Book of Angst* (Simon Spotlight) and online in *Mr. Beller's Neighborhood*. As a performer, her solo shows have appeared at various colleges across the country, as well as at the HBO Comedy Festival, the UNO Festival for Solo Performance, and the People's Improv Theatre in New York City. Barron is a host and three-time winner at *The Moth: Urban Storytelling*. She teaches humor writing at Gotham Writer's Workshop and holds a B.F.A. from NYU.

REBECCA BLOOM is an author and editor at large for *Los Angeles Confidential* magazine. A graduate of Brown University, she studied to be a chef in Paris, then changed course professionally in favor of writing. Rebecca's debut novel, *Girl Anatomy* (Harper Collins), and her second, *Tangled Up In Daydreams* (Harper Collins) were both featured in numerous national and regional publications including the *New York Times*, the *Los Angeles Times*, the *New York Post*, *In Style*, the *Hollywood Reporter*, and *Variety* in addition to various electronic outlets including *EXTRA*, *Good Day Live*, and the *Dallas Morning News*. She has just completed her third novel and can be reached at *www.rebeccabloom.com*.

⚮

ANNIE DOWNEY lives in Burlington, Vermont, with her two children, doggie, and kitties. Her work has appeared in *Hip Mama*, *UTNE Reader*, *Vermont Woman*, and *Harpers* magazine. She has also been a commentator for Vermont and National Public Radio. Currently, she is studying for her MFA in Creative Writing at Vermont College of Fine Arts. Her debut novel is *Hot and Bothered* (Algonquin Books). She can be reached at *www.hotand bothered.info* or *www.anniedowney.com*.

⚮

BENITA GOLD is the president of Benita Gold Public Relations and her eclectic client base has ranged from a neuro-oncologist to Woody Woodpecker. Benita Gold has told her dating stories in comedy clubs around New York and at the Toyota Comedy Festival and the Fringe Comedy Festival. She has written for numerous publications including *New York Magazine*, the *New York Daily News*, and *More Magazine*. Her story "My Boyfriend Peter Jennings" is currently being made into a short film.

⚏

SHARI GOLDHAGEN is a native Ohioan who holds a lot of writing degrees from Big Ten Schools in the Midwest: a journalism degree from Northwestern and an MFA from Ohio State. While writing *Family and Other Accidents*, Shari stalked celebrities for the *National Enquirer*, *Life & Style*, and *Celebrity Living Weekly*. She also received generous fellowships from Yaddo, MacDowell, and the Ohioana Library Association. Shari currently lives in New York City where she teaches fiction and works as a freelance writer. She can be reached at *www.sharigoldhagen.com*.

⚏

MELISSA PHETERSON, 28, is a freelance writer based in New Haven, CT, where she contributes to *Rochester Magazine* and iVillage .com. She has written for Salon.com, *Psychology Today*, and the *Jerusalem Post*. After graduating from Cornell University in 2001, she moved to New York City and earned a master's degree in journalism from New York University in 2005. She worked as the editor of publications for New York Presbyterian Hospital before moving to Rochester. Most recently, she served as the director of communications for the Town of Brighton, a Rochester suburb.

⧫

ANITA KAWATRA is a communications and public affairs executive in New York, specializing in crisis management and organizational turnarounds. Previously, she was a political speechwriter. She is a board member of Sanctuary for Families, the domestic violence organization, and past president of Lotus Music and Dance, the cultural organization. Anita is an adjunct professor of writing at New York University. She holds a BA from Yale College and an MA from Columbia University, where she was founding chair of the Conference on American Studies. She is working on a novel.

⧫

ADINA KAY is a nonfiction writer living in New York City. She is currently finishing her MFA at Columbia University's School of the Arts and working on a nonfiction novel about growing up and getting caught amid life, love, and landscape in New York and Jerusalem. Her creative writing has been published in the *Blood Orange Review* and *580 Split*. She loves her mother very much despite that crazy set-up.

⚜

LEORA KLEIN is a freelance writer who teaches eighth grade English in Manhattan. Her essays and articles have appeared in numerous publications, including the *New York Sun*, the *New Jersey Jewish News*, the *Pennsylvania Gazette*, and *Yad Vashem's Martyrdom and Resistance Magazine*. She received a BA from the University of Pennsylvania in English Literature and Theatre Arts and an MA in English and Comparative Literature from Columbia University. She lives in New York City and no longer accepts her parents' romantic introductions.

⚜

EVE LEDERMAN is the author of three business titles, two humorous gift books, and a memoir entitled *Letters from My Sister: On Love, Life and Hair Removal* which earned an endorsement from the the *New York Times*'s city section editor as "a warm slice of life on the edge, with an edge." (*www.LettersFromMySister.com*) She also codirected *A Good Uplift*, a short documentary about a bra shop run by a Jewish mother and son which premiered on the PBS Reel New York series in 2004. In addition, Eve performs monologues with The Moth storytelling group; she can be heard on *www.audible .com*.

⊰🎜🎝⊱

SAMANTHA LEVY, a Ph.D. candidate studying fiction at Florida State University, is originally from southern New Jersey. She received her BA in literature from Rowan University and an MA in creative writing from FSU. She is the nonfiction editor of the *Southeast Review*, and her fiction has been published in the *Chattahoochee Review*. She is currently working on her first novel and lives in Tallahassee, Florida. Samantha can be reached at *SBLevy3@aol.com*.

⊰🎜🎝⊱

JENNIFER LUDOVICI grew up in Roanoke, Virginia, where her mother currently resides. As an enthusiast of international education, she has traveled, worked, and studied in multiple countries around the world. She holds a BA in history and a master's degree in education from James Madison University. When the date in question occurred, she was the director of the study abroad and international exchange programs for Virginia Commonwealth University in Richmond, Virginia. Currently she and her husband live and work in New York City.

⁂

RACHEL PINE is the author of *The Twins of Tribeca*, a satirical novel that *Time Magazine* named to its list of "5 Fantastic First Novels." She recently contributed to the anthology *This Is Chick Lit* and the monologue show, *Love & Israel*. She is currently working on her first nonfiction project, *Dogs on Management*, a business/humor book. Pine is the senior vice president of branding and partnerships for Doubledown Media. She lives in New York City and Southampton. She can be reached at *www.rachelpine.com*.

⁂

MOLLY PRATHER is a writer and performer living in Los Angeles. She has appeared at the Upright Citizens Brigade Theater in both Los Angeles and New York in her solo show, "That Girl." As a storyteller, she is a StorySLAM winner at The Moth (Los Angeles and New York) and Spill Your Guts (UCBT LA). In 2001, she wrote and performed in the first Second City New York showcase, "We Built This City on Rent Control." In 2006, "The Hamptons Sisters" made its Off-Broadway debut, featuring Molly's book and lyrics. Molly's writing has been published in *Time Out New York*.

—⧈—

HEATHER ROBINSON is a senior writer for the *New York Daily News'* Big Town Big Heart section, in which she profiles New Yorkers who are making a difference via charitable or humanitarian work. She has also written for the *Wall Street Journal*, the *New York Post*, *New York Magazine*, *Time Out New York*, the *Philadelphia Inquirer*, and the *Los Angeles Daily News*.

—⧈—

BRENDA SCOTT ROYCE is the author of *Monkey Love* (NAL Trade), a romantic comedy about a stand-up comedienne who becomes the temporary guardian of a mischievous monkey. A former book editor, she is currently director of publications for the Los Angeles Zoo and editor of the quarterly magazine *Zoo View*. Now happily married, she looks back fondly on her myriad dating disasters and incorporates them into her fiction writing whenever possible. Her next book, *Monkey Star*, was also released by NAL Trade. Web site: *www.brendascottroyce.com*.

⌐⊐⊏⌐

RACHEL SKLAR is the media and special projects editor for the *Huffington Post* and is the editor of the site's Eat The Press page. She has contributed to the *New York Times*, the *New York Post*, the *Village Voice*, *Glamour*, *New York Magazine*, the *Financial Times*, and numerous publications in Canada. She is a frequent guest on CNN, MSNBC and Fox News. She is the author of *A Stroke of Luck: Life, Crisis and Rebirth of a Stroke Survivor* (with Howard Rocket, Canada) and *Jew-ish* (Collins). She was formerly a corporate lawyer in New York and Stockholm, where she never learned to like herring.

⌐⊐⊏⌐

ROCHELLE JEWEL SHAPIRO'S novel, *Miriam the Medium* (Simon & Schuster), was nominated for the Harold U. Ribelow Award and was published in Holland, Belgium, and the UK and is now available in paperback. She's published essays in the *New York Times* (Lives) and *Newsweek* (My Turn), and has had articles published about her in *Redbook*, the *New York Times* Long Island Section, the *Jerusalem Post*, *Jewish Week*, and others. Her poetry and short stories have appeared in many literary magazines and anthologies. She teaches Writing the Personal Essay at UCLA online and reviews books for Kirkus. She can be reached at *www.miriamthemedium.com*.

⁋

LEANNE SHEAR grew up in Buffalo, NY, attended the University of Pennsylvania in Philadelphia, and now resides in New York City, where she is a writer and master's degree candidate (studying Politics and Culture) at NYU. *The Perfect Manhattan*—a novel she coauthored with Tracey Toomey—is loosely based on their experiences bartending in Manhattan and the Hamptons and highlights some of the class and societal issues they encountered while straddling the fence between the working and "glamour" classes (*http://www.theperfectmanhattan.com*). Their second book, *Cocktail Therapy*, was released by Simon Spotlight Entertainment. Leanne has also written for such eclectic publications as *New York Magazine*, *City Limits*, PopandPolitics.com, *WireTap*, *Glamour*, and *Life & Style*.

⁋

HEMMY SO is a staff writer at the *South Florida Sun-Sentinel*. She has written for the *Los Angeles Times*, the *Poughkeepsie Journal*, *New York Observer*, and *Yin Magazine*. Prior to becoming a journalist, she worked as an attorney. She is a graduate of Rice University and New York University School of Law.

⊰⊱

TRACEY TOOMEY graduated from NYU's Tisch School of the Arts before appearing on *All My Children*, *Law and Order: SVU*, and in several films and theater productions. Along with her writing partner, Leanne Shear, she coauthored the novel, *The Perfect Manhattan*; the nonfiction advice book, *Cocktail Therapy*; and the essay "Girls Can Do Anything" in the anthology *It's a Wonderful Lie: The Truth About Life in Your Twenties*. Currently she freelances at *Life & Style*, *Runner's World*, and *Glamour*, and writes the Imbibe column for *Hamptons Magazine*. She can be reached at *www.theperfectmanhattan.com* or *www.givemecocktailtherapy.com*.

⊰⊱

AURY WALLINGTON's television writing credits include *Sex and the City* and *Veronica Mars*. Her novel, *POP!* (Razorbill Books), was named one of the New York Public Library's 2007 Books for the Teen Age. Aury lives in Los Angeles with her dog, Tuesday. Visit her Web site at *www.aurywallington.com*.

KATHERINE WESSLING has been everything from a bicycle courier to a fashion stylist at a magazine, but she's happiest when she's writing or acting. Her personal essays have been published in *Swing* and *Speak* magazines and heard on WNYC's broadcast of NPR's *Morning Edition*. She's written various other bits and pieces for *Marie Claire, CosmoGirl, Elle* (UK), *Town & Country, Good Housekeeping, (ai) performance for the planet,* and *Plumb*. She also wrote the young reader's book, *Backstage at a Movie Set*. Katherine's short plays have been produced in New York City, where she's lived for many years.

About the Editor

ALIX STRAUSS is a media satirist and lifestyle trend writer. She has appeared on national morning shows and talk shows including ABC, CBS, CNN, and VH1. She has written for the *New York Times*, the *New York Post*, and the *Daily News*, as well as national magazines *Time Magazine*, *Town & Country Travel*, *Marie Claire*, *Entertainment Weekly*, *Self*, *Men's Health*, and *Esquire*, among others. Her collection of shorts, *The Joy of Funerals* (St. Martin's Press) won the Ingram Award and was named Best Debut Novel by the *New York Resident*. Alix's fiction has appeared in the *Primavera Literary Journal*, *Hampton Shorts Literary Journal*, the *Idaho Review*, *Quality Women's Fiction*, the *Blue Moon Café III*, and *A Kudzu Christmas*. Her short story, "Shrinking Away," won the David Dornstein Creative Writing Award. *The Joy of Funerals* will be heading to the big screen with Stockard Channing attached to direct. Alix will write the screenplay as well. She can be reached at *www.joyoffunerals.com* or *www.alixstrauss.com*.